Speaking from V

For Rebecca
With very best
wishes on your
ordination as
a deacon.
Kevin

SPEAKING from WITHIN

BIBLICAL APPROACHES FOR EFFECTIVE PREACHING

KIERAN J. O'MAHONY OSA

VERITAS

A word fitly spoken is
like apples of gold in a setting of silver.
(Prov 25:11)

'The word is near you, on your lips and in your heart'
(that is, the word of faith that we proclaim);
because if you confess with your lips that Jesus is Lord
and believe in your heart that God raised him from the dead,
you will be saved.
(Rm 10:8-9)

Preparation for preaching requires love.
We only devote periods of quiet time
to the things or the people whom we love;
and here we are speaking of the God whom we love,
a God who wishes to speak to us.
Because of this love,
we can take as much time as we need,
like every true disciple:
'Speak, Lord, for your servant is listening' (1 Sm 3:9).
(*The Joy of the Gospel* §146)

The Bible tells of God's relationship with God's people through
the centuries.
This record always needs to be interpreted
in the context of the Church's faith, prayer and worship,
and in such a way that what scripture said for its original
audience is faithfully re-expressed for the modern world.[1]

---

1. http://ireland.anglican.org/information/10.

Dedication

To the Dean and Chapter of St Patrick's Cathedral, Dublin,
in gratitude for the witness of faith and for their generous
hospitality during my time as ecumenical canon.

Published 2016 by Veritas Publications
7–8 Lower Abbey Street
Dublin 1, Ireland
publications@veritas.ie
www.veritas.ie

ISBN 978 1 84730 654 8

10 9 8 7 6 5 4 3 2 1

Chapters One and Two originally appeared as a single chapter entitled 'Speaking From Within: More Effective Preaching', in *Priesthood Today: Ministry in a Changing Church*, Eamonn Conway, ed. (Dublin: Veritas, 2013), pp. 336–46. That essay has been adjusted for this volume.

Chapter Three will be included, in a somewhat different form, in a new collection of essays to be published under the auspices of the Irish Biblical Association, with the provisional title *The Bible in Ireland* (2017).

A catalogue record for this book is available from the British Library.

Cover designed by Heather Costello, Veritas Publications
Printed in the Republic of Ireland by SPRINT-print Ltd, Dublin

Veritas books are printed on paper made from the wood pulp of managed forests. For every tree felled, at least one tree is planted, thereby renewing natural resources.

Contents

Foreword

Anyone who preaches is aware that the art of the homily is both ephemeral and precarious. It is ephemeral: after all, if it is not for the day, then when is it for? It is also precarious: often it is not the homily we consider good that is the most effective – on the contrary, fragile preaching, in all its tentativeness, can touch the hearers far more effectively. Preaching is also a long-term project. No one imagines that each homily speaks to most or even many of the congregation. A good homily is grounded in the faith, rooted in the scriptures, reflects on life in general, and addresses contemporary thought and experience in particular. The cumulative effect of such integrated preaching lays a foundation of faith and even an expectation, so that when the hearer's time of need arises, he or she will know where to turn.

So why another book on preaching? It may be best to start with what this book is not. It is not another handbook or manual on preaching. This is already extraordinarily well served by books such as that of Bishop Ken Untener in his *Preaching Better*.[1] I recommend this book heartily.

The present work does not try to repeat in less lively language what Pope Francis achieved in *Evangelii Gaudium: The Joy of the Gospel*. The substantial Chapter Three of that letter, devoted specifically to the proclamation of the Gospel, includes most encouraging words on the homily in the context of the liturgy (§135–144) as well as detailed advice on preparing the homily (§145–159). Pope Francis does practise what he preaches; his short, profound homilies are rooted in the biblical text and, at

---

1. Ken Untener, *Preaching Better: Practical Suggestions for Homilists* (Mahwah, NJ: Paulist Press, 1999). It is still in print and there is even a Kindle edition. This book is about the best you could imagine in terms of the practical preparation, delivery and critique of the homily.

the same time, speak to contemporary issues in the language of today. Everyone who preaches would do well to be familiar with *The Joy of the Gospel* and to take it to heart. Speaking in a pastoral mode that does not lack directness, Francis writes:

> Preparation for preaching is so important a task that a prolonged time of study, prayer, reflection and pastoral creativity should be devoted to it. With great affection I wish to stop for a moment and offer a method of preparing homilies. Some may find these suggestions self-evident, but I consider it helpful to offer them as a way of emphasising the need to devote quality time to this precious ministry. Some pastors argue that such preparation is not possible given the vast number of tasks which they must perform; nonetheless, I presume to ask that each week a sufficient portion of personal and community time be dedicated to this task, *even if less time has to be given to other important activities*. Trust in the Holy Spirit who is at work during the homily and is not merely passive but active and creative. It demands that we offer ourselves and all our abilities as instruments (cf. Rm 12:1) which God can use. A preacher who does not prepare is not 'spiritual'; he is dishonest and irresponsible with the gifts he has received. (The Joy of the Gospel, §145; emphasis added.)

In other words, there is no need to repeat what has been so well said originally! Changing wine into water is not what we are about.

Personally, I am convinced that both prayerful and critical reflection on the faith is needed more than ever. When expressed like that, no one could be against it. What I am really saying, however, is that all preaching is a form of theology, whether we admit it or not. After all, what is theology? Theology is the critical dialogue between lived faith and contemporary life. The goal of theology is to promote the growth of believers so that our lives are integrated spiritually, practically and intellectually. Because of previous bad practice, some speakers avoid intellectualising when preaching, under the guise of keeping it simple. Alas, simple can all too often devolve into simplistic.

Allow me to make two comments. First, there is no avoiding theology. It is only a question of good or bad theology, or less good or less bad theology. Second, the single greatest weakness of traditional Irish Christianity has been the lack of a critical understanding of the faith. The evidence for this is the way people walk away from the faith, apparently with no awareness or regret that they abandon something rich, engaging, exciting and deep. The level of conversation regarding aspects of the faith, at least in public discourse, is at the low end of the spectrum. There's no point in finding who is to blame – there's enough of that in our society. The high rates of abandoning faith are certainly a cause for concern and worth trying to understand. It would, however, be a subject for another book.

The homily, on the other hand, is a unique opportunity to explore the reasonableness of faith. By reasonableness I do not mean that faith may be reduced to what can be achieved rationally.[2] I mean, rather, that faith and reason do not fundamentally contradict each other. To repeat – our goal is the integration of faith and life, and that integration includes my understanding. One of the best books on preaching as theology is *Excited to Speak, Exciting to Hear: The Art of Preaching*,[3] by John Bodycomb, a minister in the Uniting Church of Australia. The title alone says it all. Unfortunately, this book, which adventurously explores the dialogue between faith, biblical

---

2. G.K. Chesterton's observation comes to mind: 'The madman is not the man who has lost his reason. The madman is the man who has lost *everything except his reason.*' (Emphasis added.)

3. John Bodycomb, *Excited to Speak, Exciting to Hear: The Art of Preaching* (Adelaide: OpenBook Publishers, 2003).

studies and contemporary culture, is no longer in print (not even in Google Books). The good news is that Bodycomb has written another book, a kind of spiritual autobiography, which covers similar critical issues of faith for today, entitled *No Fixed Address: Faith as Journey*.[4] Again, the title is eloquent.

I hope my own title also says it all. The only preaching worth attending to is the word that comes from within. This book explores 'from within' in several ways. The first chapter is really an encouragement for preparation in prayer (*lectio divina*) and through consistent reflection. Only from within that personal encounter can we hope that a word of life will be spoken. The second chapter is devoted to the preparation of the homily, after the time in prayer.

In our tradition, we use a lectionary. Like all such selections, it is an interpretation of sorts, with evident strengths and clear weaknesses. A familiarity with the purpose, sequence and potential of the selections offered is simply a professional requirement. The lectionary is decisively not just one biblical passage after another. There is a structure and an overall plan, especially in the festal seasons. It is incumbent upon the preacher to know how the lectionary 'works' so he or she can also speak 'from within' the readings offered, as an integrated whole. It is good news that the churches of the Reformation have adopted and adapted the Roman Lectionary. Largely, we are reading the same scripture passages each Sunday; this facilitates sharing of resources and even homily preparation.

The fourth chapter takes this image of 'from within' a step further. The cumbersome title should be 'Creating a Personal Biblical Culture'. By that I mean that the preacher should gradually become a skilled and competent reader of the

---

4. John Bodycomb, *No Fixed Address: Faith as Journey* (Richmond, VA: Spectrum Publications, 2010).

scriptures, based on prayer, familiarity, love and study. Pope Francis is, again, a good example. He knows his Bible and, while not a biblical scholar, he brings to bear a richness that comes from years of attentiveness, prayer and penetrating reflection. He is an example of how we should all be.

In the last three chapters, the book switches tack and presents three scenes from the Gospel according to Luke. These somewhat more detailed studies are offered as an illustration – it is hoped – of the value of going a bit deeper into the Word of God. The 'within' this time becomes within scripture and within the richness of biblical studies. There's no doubting that biblical studies can reach a high technical level. Nevertheless, I remain convinced that the really valuable insights are also communicable and can be expressed in language that the ordinary person may grasp. To facilitate such reflection in these last chapters, I have added at the end some pointers for reflection and a prayer taken from the ICEL collection entitled *Opening Prayers*.[5]

Finally, for whom is this book intended? It is aimed predominantly at those who preach, but also those who hand on the faith in any way. It is also my hope that the ordinary believer could pick it up and find it useful. The advice on *lectio divina* in the first chapter would be the starting point for such a person.

5. International Commission for English in the Liturgy (ICEL), *Opening Prayers: Collects in a Contemporary Language – Scripture Related Prayers for Sundays and Holy Days, Years A, B and C* (Norwich: Canterbury Press, 2001). This collection of prayers, inspired by God's Word, is very inspiring and of great practical use for getting to the heart of the readings. It can be ordered directly from Canterbury Press. The product description is accurate: 'This much-praised and strikingly beautiful collection of prayers offers a satisfying resource to all who are looking for collects in a contemporary idiom. Dramatic in their imagery, richly biblical in their language and skilfully connecting the Bible readings for the day, they will enrich worship by focusing hearts and minds on the scriptures read in church – and all this in a style which resonates authentically with the longings and hopes of these seeking God in today's world. Clergy and worship leaders in many denominations now using the three-year lectionary will gladly welcome this splendid collection which includes prayers for every Sunday, holy day and major festivals of Years A, B and C.'

I do hope it goes beyond the traditional boundaries between the Churches. As an elected Ecumenical Canon of St Patrick's Cathedral, Dublin, I have known nothing but welcome and fraternity and a profound sense of common purpose. Precisely on account of that, this modest work is dedicated to the Dean and Chapter.

1
The Word as Place of Encounter

To interpret a biblical text, we need to be patient, to put aside all other concerns, and to give it our time, interest and undivided attention. We must leave aside any other pressing concerns and create an environment of serene concentration. It is useless to attempt to read a biblical text if all we are looking for are quick, easy and immediate results. Preparation for preaching requires love. We only devote periods of quiet time to the things or the people whom we love; and here we are speaking of the God whom we love, a God who wishes to speak to us. Because of this love, we can take as much time as we need, like every true disciple: 'Speak, Lord, for your servant is listening' (1 Sm 3:9). (*The Joy of the Gospel*, §146)

The use of the Bible has been strongly promoted, at least at official level, since the Council of Trent.[1] In one of its earliest Decrees on Reformation, that Council stated that every diocese should have on its staff a biblical scholar for the better understanding of the scriptures among the clergy. Vatican II and many subsequent documents have promoted both the Bible and biblical studies, encouraging insistently and warmly the increased use of the Bible for prayer, for pastoral life, for liturgy and so forth. One of the encouraging signs is the increased awareness of the importance of the Word of God among the people of God. In some sense, the formal encouragement since Vatican II seems finally to have found a place in people's own journey of faith. We take up scripture no longer because we ought to, but because we want to. We want to because the regeneration of the Church can have no other genesis than in the Word of God. As Erasmus put it, years before the Council of Trent, in the introduction to his Greek New Testament: '[it] will bring you the living image of Christ's holy mind and the speaking, healing, dying, rising Christ himself, and thus render him so fully present that you see less if you gazed upon him with your own eyes.'[2] The move

---

1. J. O'Malley, *Trent: What Happened at the Council* (London: Harvard University Press, 2013), pp. 99–102. See also the Decrees of Trent, Fifth Session, Decree on Reformation, Part 1, which in part reads: 'On the Institution of a Lectureship of Sacred Scripture, and of the liberal arts. The same sacred and holy Synod, adhering to the pious constitutions of the Sovereign Pontiffs, and of approved councils, and embracing and adding to them; that the heavenly treasure of the sacred books, which the Holy Ghost has with the greatest liberality delivered unto men, may not lie neglected, hath ordained and decreed, that – in those churches where there is found to be a prebend, prestimony, or other stipend under whatsoever name, destined for lecturers in sacred theology – the bishops, archbishops, primates, and other Ordinaries of those places shall force and compel, even by the substraction of the fruits, those who hold such prebend, prestimony, or stipend, to expound and interpret the said sacred Scripture, either personally, if they be competent, or otherwise by a competent substitute, to be chosen by the said bishops, archbishops, primates, and other Ordinaries of those places. But, for the future, let not such prebend, prestimony, or stipend be bestowed save on competent persons, and those who can themselves discharge that office; and otherwise let the provision made be null and void.'

2. Ibid., p. 43

from the ideal to the real, from official, formal endorsement to real hunger of the heart is indeed a beam of light and hope in the current darkness of the Church.

In many parishes across the country there are Bible study and *lectio divina* groups. If these groups are paying attention to the lectionary, their hearing of the Word on Sundays is greatly enhanced by their familiarity with the readings of each week. There is a corresponding raising of expectations when it comes to the guidance of those in ministry and, in a special way, a raising of expectations regarding the homily. Not everyone, of course, but certainly some are really hungry for the Word. We expect from now on a responsible and informed presentation of God's Word for that particular Sunday. How can that be encouraged and enabled?

The title of this reflection indicates the direction of the content: speaking from within. Speaking from within means speaking from *inside* our own experience, both my experience of life and my experience of praying the scriptures. One of the pluses of *lectio* is that it brings together experience, the Word of God and study. There are many different way of praying the scripture and certainly many ways of conducting *lectio*. The destination is always the same, but the route will vary. I would like to describe one such route, fully aware that it may not suit everyone.

Before preaching on the Word of God, the preacher begins by listening to the Word. This can open very simply: a set place and time, a moment of quiet, perhaps some reflective music and certainly a prayer. For example:

Merciful God, anoint me with your Holy Spirit. As I read your Word, let me hear your voice speaking to me from within. Give me wisdom to understand your message to me. Let your word be the joy of my heart and a lamp for my steps. May I rejoice in the blessedness of those who hear your Word and keep it. Speak, Lord, your servant is listening ...

For the first step in this prayer of listening, take up the passage you wish to pray and read it slowly. In the following silence, pay attention to how you feel as you hear the word. There are three worlds at play here, the world before the text (yourself and your concerns), the world behind the text (the context and background) and the world in the text (whatever it is saying). It is important to begin with where you are and how you feel. When the various steps of reflection have been undertaken, the hope is that you will have heard a word that addresses your experience, a word that will penetrate your heart and take you further on the road of conversion and discipleship. Letting the Word resonate with your personal experience takes time and the moment should not be rushed. Let the Word summon up feelings, memories, images – really anything at all in your own life that is evoked by the images and events in the scripture passage.

Only after adequate time has been devoted to the first step should the second be taken. This time, we read the passage explicitly for understanding. Read it again slowly and notice whatever is not clear to you. This could be anything: a word; a custom; some historical background; the religious teaching of the passage as a whole. It is very useful at this point to have more than one translation at your disposal. The version in the lectionary is the first edition of the Jerusalem Bible, which has itself since been updated to the New Jerusalem Bible. A very popular current translation is the New Revised Standard Version, especially in its study edition, the HarperCollins Study Bible. The notes and essays are excellent. Occasionally, however, the laudable desire for inclusive language can obscure the original sense. There is yet another translation called the New English

Bible, with very complete notes. It can be viewed at https://bible.org and offers a fine translation[3] with comprehensive explanatory notes. Finally, a version for 'these islands' is the Revised English Bible, a version that never seems to have received the recognition and use it deserved. In any case, it is good to have more than one translation, given that the majority of preachers will not be reading in the original languages.

At this point we encounter two other 'worlds' of the text, the world behind it and the world within it. Both are important. Today there are many methods and approaches, conveniently summarised and assessed in *The Interpretation of the Bible in the Church* (1993). For Catholics and other traditions convinced of the coherence of faith and reason, the historical critical method (really a collection of methods) poses challenges but no threat to our faithful reading of the Bible. In the words of Pontifical Biblical Commission:

> The historical critical method is the indispensable method for the scientific study of the meaning of ancient texts. Holy Scripture, inasmuch as it is the 'Word of God in human language', has been composed by human authors in all its various parts and in all the sources that lie behind them. Because of this, its proper understanding not only admits the use of this method *but actually requires it.* (§1A; emphasis added.)

This means that it is incumbent upon the preacher to be adequately informed about the text, its context and meaning. This does not have to be burdensome scholarship; it is sufficient to use standard resources regularly and well. Naïve interpretations, which take no account of historical questions and literary forms, serve no one. Just how many 75cc bottles of probably low alcohol wine were produced at Cana is well and truly beside

---

3. The NET version is excellent for reading the letters of St Paul.

the point. Furthermore, my own extensive experience in adult faith formation leads me to the conclusion that many people are ready for something more grown-up than that. Simple doesn't have to mean simplistic.

A good study Bible with decent notes will satisfy many questions. Any of the standard one-volume dictionaries of the Bible would also be very serviceable. As a larger general resource it would be really hard to beat *The New Interpreter's Dictionary of the Bible*. It is certainly comprehensive, in five volumes, but also pastorally accessible. In fact, it was written with the pastoral use of the Bible in mind and so, while wholly academic, it is never forbidding or obfuscating.

It is good to remember that such informing of oneself is always at the service of prayerful listening and practical preaching and never just for its own sake. We return, in a spirit of prayer, to the text once more. It should be read slowly – as always – with a view to noticing how I myself, at this moment in my life, find myself addressed by the reading. This is quite a personal moment and its importance cannot be overstated. One could develop some 'pointers for prayer', that is, possible directions for reflection that suggest themselves. At this point, after about an hour or perhaps slightly more, it would be good to stop. The suggestion here is that you might return to the passage for a period each day for the next couple of days. A practical way of doing this may be to schedule it as part of your regular prayer so that it does not become 'lost'. The Word of God really is alive and active, and it is surprising how our reading of a passage changes and grows, even over only a few days. Towards the end of that time, two more steps are proposed.

The penultimate step is to read the passage once more, slowly, and in the silence that follows spend time reviewing what came up for you over the last few days of reflection. How different was your final reflection from your first? Did any particular point emerge as a special word for you personally at this moment? It would be useful to keep some kind of diary or note of your reactions because that would help in appropriating even more fully whatever it was that may have emerged.

The very last step is really a moment of prayer or better prayerful contemplation. It would be appropriate to read the passage one more time, as a direct way of entering a prayer moment. This moment of final reflection could be verbal – using words and phrases from the Gospel. In particular, a prayer of thanksgiving for the Good News in the passage fits in here. As we harvest the extended reflection, the time of quiet leads naturally to a moment of simply being in God's presence, in whom we live and move and have our being. As the reader will have noticed, this kind of prayer is not mere homily preparation, but a regular and nourishing part of the life of prayer as such. This is intentional. The risk among 'professional' readers of the scriptures is a certain instrumentalisation of the Word of God. If we as preachers are to have a word of life for those who hear us, we ourselves must have heard that word of life to begin with. Hence the title of this chapter: speaking from within – that is, from within my own encounter with the Lord through his living Word.

2
Writing the Homily

Some people think they can be good preachers because they know what ought to be said, but they pay no attention to how it should be said, that is, the concrete way of constructing a sermon. They complain when people do not listen to or appreciate them, but perhaps they have never taken the trouble to find the proper way of presenting their message. Let us remember that 'the obvious importance of the content of evangelisation must not overshadow the importance of its ways and means'. Concern for the way we preach is likewise a profoundly spiritual concern. It entails responding to the love of God by putting all our talents and creativity at the service of the mission which he has given us; at the same time, it shows a fine, active love of neighbour by refusing to offer others a product of poor quality. In the Bible, for example, we can find advice on how to prepare a homily so as to best to reach people: 'Speak concisely, say much in few words' (Eccles [Sir] 32:8). (*The Joy of the Gospel*, §156)

It is standard practice to distinguish between a sermon (a talk on a given subject) and a homily (a reflection closely based on the readings). Our word homily comes from the Greek verb *homilia/ homilein*. Its meaning is captured in these passages in Luke–Acts:

> Now on that same day two of them were going to a village called Emmaus, about seven miles from Jerusalem, and talking [homilein] with each other about all these things that had happened. While they were talking [homilein] and discussing, Jesus himself came near and went with them, but their eyes were kept from recognising him. And he said to them, 'What are you discussing with each other while you walk along?' (Luke 24:13-17)

> Then Paul went upstairs, and after he had broken bread and eaten, he continued to converse [homilein] with them until dawn; then he left. (Acts 20:11)

> At the same time he (Felix) hoped that money would be given him by Paul, and for that reason he used to send for him very often and converse [homilein] with him. (Acts 24:26)

The range of meanings of this verb are: to be in a group and speak, to speak, to converse, to address. The associated noun (*homilia*) is close in meaning: to be in a state of close association with others, to engage in talk, either as conversation, speech or lecture. The classical root means to be in company with, to consort with (from the adjective *homos* meaning one and the same, common, joint).

This brief excursus into etymology serves to remind us that a homily means in a particular way 'to be with others' and that it should be natural, as natural as having a conversation. This does not mean, however, that it needs no preparation or presentation. Such illusions from the seventies – perhaps in reaction to the stylised or somewhat theatrical preaching of the past – constitute the myth of spontaneity, as if only what is spontaneous or casual is authentic. A comparison with music may help to make the point. Nothing sounds more natural than the music of Mozart. As you listen you feel this is the only way this music can be. At the same time, nothing is more full of artifice than such music, carefully calibrated with astonishing, though concealed, sophistication, with the result that it sounds 'natural' on an altogether other plane. In that sense, artifice (that is, skilful preparation and presentation) does not at all mean artificial or lacking in genuineness. The end result will indeed be 'conversation', but with a direction and a structure not usually found in casual conversation. With this brief plea for the art of preaching, let us move to the preparation of the homily, bearing in mind that the preparation cannot be separated from the encounter with the Lord in prayer and reading.

The first and most important step is to figure out what it is that needs to be said in this situation. This means knowing the congregation really well and what is affecting their lives, what is 'going on' for them. Nothing is more important than this first effort to reflect. After all, the hope is to deliver a word of life in a particular context. The preacher has to know this context before anything else. In this regard, a really good example is St Paul. Before dictating any of his letters, he first of all informs himself thoroughly. One example may suffice:

> But Timothy has just now come to us from you, and has brought us the good news of your faith and love. He has told us also that you always remember us kindly and long to see us – just as we long to see you. For this reason, brothers and sisters, during all our distress and persecution we have been encouraged about you through your faith. For we now live, if you continue to stand firm in the Lord. (1 Th 3:6-8)

Often when presenting his teaching, St Paul uses the shorthand or slogans of the groups he confronts ('It is well for a man not to touch a woman') as a measure of just how well informed he is about the situation of which he speaks. Of course, it may well be that over all the Sundays of the year there is nothing particularly dramatic happening in the faith community (a welcome prospect in these difficult times). Often, however, there are things happening in the community, or even *to* the community, in the wider society, things that provide the link between the Word of God and life today. The image of the great Karl Barth preparing his sermons with the Bible in one hand and newspaper in the other (while the 'divine Mozart' sounded in the background) comes to mind. Otherwise, we may find ourselves speaking into the air (1 Cor 14:9)!

Having landed on the core topic or context that needs to be addressed, the next step is to provide a sequence that is engaging and interesting. Without wishing to be prescriptive, I would suggest the following moments, each meriting distinct consideration.

Beginning a Homily

All beginnings are important, and so the opening couple of sentences need to be carefully chosen and calibrated. There are two goals here. The first is to get people's attention, for without that you will indeed be speaking into the air[1] or, worse, to yourself! An anecdote, a personal story or something you have observed may serve to get started. The second goal is to get people, so to speak, on your side, so that they will want to listen to what you are about to say. The key here is brevity and wit. A long introduction may not simply delay engagement with the

---

1. So with yourselves; if in a tongue you utter speech that is not intelligible, how will anyone know what is being said? For you will be speaking into the air (1 Cor 14:9).

main issue, it may even obscure it. Sometimes, however, to set the scene, a sequence of events or preliminary considerations may need to be offered.

The Main Point

In any case, at the end of the introduction, it would serve both the homilist and the hearers if the preacher could offer in one simple sentence whatever it is (s)he wants to get across. This does not have to be complete – that would be to risk tedium by saying it all at the start – but it does have to be clear and serviceable. This could be a question or an observation or an apparent paradox. Some such one-liner early on in the homily would be an act of mercy towards all concerned! Again, St Paul is a good example. For in instance, in 1 Thessalonians 1:9-10 he gives the message of the letter in a nutshell, to be unfolded in detail over the next five chapters.

Argument(s)

The word argument is used here in the positive sense of reasons for thinking such and such might be the case. Preaching is designed to persuade, and persuasion is achieved chiefly by argument and evidence. The current preaching style (if there be such!) may again be a reaction to desiccated theological sermons of old and that is understandable. However, a reaction that deprives the homily of ideas would be extreme. Most people can handle a degree of sophistication these days. A more common risk in homilies is to go down the route of mere exhortation, without adducing arguments or evidence. In the end, this depends more on forceful presentation and personality rather than on reasoned conviction. There is a further risk: moral exhortation places the speaker in the role of judge and the hearers can feel they are being judged. When people feel they are being morally assessed in some way, they do pay attention, but the distancing effect of assessment may cause them to withhold consent and receptivity. As Nivard Kinsella once said, 'If you haven't discovered by the age of thirty-five that you should be better ... forget it!'

Whatever kinds of ideas and arguments we do bring to bear, they serve the unfolding of the Word as the preacher encountered it in prayer. The lectionary, for all its imperfections, does provide a rich vein of teaching and experience, to be mined Sunday after Sunday. To feed people with our own ideas is not such a good idea after all.

Arguments can be of many kinds. Certainly, one can use scientific evidence wherever appropriate. For example, in the case of care for the earth, the catastrophic melting of the polar icecaps could be striking and relevant. Or, when addressing values and attitudes in society, polls and surveys can help. For example, it emerged in a recent survey that 17 per cent of Australians think Jesus never existed. Evidence from developmental psychology can be very helpful in dealing with stages of life and faith.

There are also arguments from personal experience – some personal context, in which a particular insight came to mind. Such 'I witness' can be powerful indeed and usually holds people's attention. Depending on whom you are speaking to, recent illustrations from films (Pat Collins' *Silence,* for instance) or novels (even *Harry Potter*, appealing both to children and adults) or occasionally a phrase from poetry can be penetrating.

From time to time, it would be good to attempt a more biblically focused homily. This would most likely not work all the time, but certainly it could be effective on occasion. An example might be paying attention to the special use of the word compassion in the Gospels – used exclusively of Jesus or of God in the parables. This can throw light on its use in the Parable of the Prodigal Son. Or take a word like *shalom*, which means something rather more in its biblical wealth of resonance than our pedestrian peace of mind. Narrative is always appealing, and so an example from other places and times can be constructive.

Challenging common unexamined presuppositions in our contemporary culture is needed today. The prophetic word is there to disturb and destabilise. We do live in a culture of distraction, a culture that tends to close out time for reflection on the things that really matter. The 'dis-ease' can be deeper. In a postmodern frame, there can lurk a conviction that there is no point whatsoever in looking at the deeper questions, a kind of counsel of despair, a conviction that chance and absurdity are the marks of human existence. The hunger for something more is part of the spiritual DNA of being human. The biblical picture of God, both faithful and true, could not be more different.[2]

One could go on, but the point has been made that the conversation, which the homily is, should engage more than the heart of the believer. Only abstractly can we separate mind and heart: we can feel our thoughts and we can think our feelings.

At the centre of our faith stands the person of Jesus and his Good News. The different arguments brought to bear lead eventually to some faith affirmation precisely about Jesus and his teaching. These words of Benedict XVI retain their significance:

---

2. For our dialogue with the times, I have found these recent books especially useful. John Cottingham, *Why Believe* (London: Continuum, 2015); *How to Believe* (London: Continuum, 2009); Rupert Shortt, *God is No Thing* (London: C. Hurst & Co., 2016); Terry Eagleton, *Reason, Faith and Revolution* (Yale University Press: New Haven and London, 2009); Elizabeth A. Johnson, *Ask the Beasts: Darwin and the God of Love* (London: Continuum, 2014); Francis Spufford, *Unapologetic: Why, despite everything, Christianity can still make surprising emotional sense* (London: Faber & Faber, 2012). All of these are conveniently available on Kindle.

Being Christian is not the result of an ethical choice or a lofty idea, but the encounter with an event, a person, which gives life a new horizon and a decisive direction. (*God is Love* §1)

In the end, all our preaching should bring the hearers to a renewed and deeper encounter with the Risen Lord, and to a deeper and renewed discipleship. The quality of relationship, of encounter, of horizon, of direction, this is what is at stake. There is no need for homilies to be the last word on anything; they are part of a longer conversation and that conversation or homilia is a being with others and with Jesus, which transcends the particular occasion.

Concluding a Homily

Every oral communication requires a conclusion, the purpose of which is threefold: to get the attention of the hearers yet again, to summarise what has been said, and to touch the hearts of all assembled. The summary can again be a sentence or two to pull it all together. There are many wonderful summaries in Paul. Again, one example may suffice:

Welcome one another, therefore, just as Christ has welcomed you, for the glory of God. For I tell you that Christ has become a servant of the circumcised on behalf of the truth of God in order that he might confirm the promises given to the patriarchs, and in order that the Gentiles might glorify God for his mercy. (Rm 15:7-9 NRSV)

Careful examination reveals that the grand sweep of Romans is summarised intellectually and yet presented practically and emotionally in these few words. A homily should leave people slightly unsettled, their minds not quite at rest.

As a practical guide to clarity in communication, I suggest, therefore, the following outline:

1. **Introduction:** to raise people's attention and interest.
2. **Main message:** in one sentence, fairly early on (it can be repeated in the conclusion, with some added enrichment).
3. **Arguments:** the goal is persuasion by combining conviction and reason.
4. **Conclusion:** to summarise, to encourage and unsettle.

Rigid adherence to such a schema would be artificial and constricting. At the same time, being aware of what you are trying to achieve in the different moments will help clarify both for the speaker and the hearers. Often, the best effect is achieved by cutting out whatever clutters up or obscures the main line of the presentation. One plus of computers is that such good ideas can be kept for use at another time.

Writing and Delivering the Homily

A homily, however brief, will benefit from the discipline of writing. It helps to see the ideas in their actual sequence. It is also an opportunity to eliminate awkward expressions or to dispense with any technical terms that may put people off. Much of the energy of preaching is and should be given over to finding new language for faith convictions. In many cases, the old language lost its resonance long ago. A simple example would be the word redemption. Does it mean anything to people today? We all hear and use clichés all of the time ('singing off the same hymn sheet'), but at heart clichés are evidence of laziness. Writing also affords an opportunity to make language more attractive and appealing.

Finally, while we do indeed write out our homilies (or these days carry them to the pulpit on our tablets), nevertheless effective communication means eye contact. For a real *homilia* or conversation with real people, nothing can replace speaking directly and with conviction. This really means committing to memory what you are going to say. Occasionally, for more formal or more difficult occasions, a homily may of course be read, but for the ordinary Sunday the preacher should look at the listeners gathered around the Word. While we cannot and need not take on the high quality of communication in the media, people are accustomed to such quality communication. For the sake of the Gospel and for the sake of our fellow believers, we owe them our best. Such memorisation is not the be all and end all of good preaching: a listener of mine once commented that even homilies that are not read sound read, nevertheless. Sometimes you really can't win! The habit of praying the text, with its gradual 'harvesting' of teachings over a week or so should be a good help in memorising because it will be based on my own experience of the biblical passage.

By Way of Conclusion

Our topic is one dimension of a larger project: handing on the faith. Evangelisation – to give it its formal name – is central to the life and well-being of the Christian community.[3] Preaching is only one aspect of catechesis/evangelisation, but it is an important, very regular part. It takes time and considerable personal engagement. The benefit of good preaching is enormous in the life of God's people. It is not that everyone goes away every Sunday newly informed and on fire. Rather, gradually, Sunday after Sunday, the hearers are convinced of the Good News, that it makes sense and that it connects to life. When their time of need arises, they will know where to turn.

---

3. Pierre Hegy, *Wake up, Lazarus* (Bloomington: iUniverse, 2011).

3

The Worshipping Community and the Lectionary

It is worth remembering that 'the liturgical proclamation of the word of God, especially in the Eucharistic assembly, is not so much a time for meditation and catechesis as a dialogue between God and his people, a dialogue in which the great deeds of salvation are proclaimed and the demands of the covenant are continually restated.' The homily has special importance due to its Eucharistic context: it surpasses all forms of catechesis as the supreme moment in the dialogue between God and his people which lead up to sacramental communion. The homily takes up once more the dialogue which the Lord has already established with his people. The preacher must know the heart of his community, in order to realise where its desire for God is alive and ardent, as well as where that dialogue, once loving, has been thwarted and is now barren. (*The Joy of the Gospel*, §137)

Introduction

On 6 April 2014, the Bishop of Rome did something that would perhaps have surprised some of his predecessors: he distributed copies of the Gospel to all present in St Peter's Square. The gift was accompanied by the following words:

> I would now like to make a simple gesture for you. Over the last few Sundays, I suggested that you should all acquire a small copy of the Gospel, to have with you during the day, to be able to take it out frequently. Then I remembered the old tradition of the Church whereby, during Lent, the Gospel was handed over to those preparing for Baptism. Today I would like to offer to you who are present in St Peter's Square – but as a token to everyone – a pocket Gospel. It will be given out for free. There are set places in the Square for distributing the text. I can see a few from here. Go up to one of those places and take the Gospel. Take it and carry it with you and read it every day: it is Jesus himself who speaks within. It is the word of Jesus: this is the word of Jesus.

> It is he who says to you: you have received at no cost, give at no cost. Give the message of the Gospel. Perhaps someone cannot believe that it really is for free. 'How much is it? What should I pay, Father?' Let's make a deal: in exchange for this gift, do some act of charity, a gesture of gratuitous love, a prayer for your adversaries, a reconciliation, anything …

These days you can read the Gospel using all sorts of gadgets. You can can have the whole Bible on your mobile or tablet. What matters is to read the word of God, in whatever medium, but read the word of God: it is Jesus who speaks to us there. Welcome that word with an open heart because the good seed will bear fruit.

There is even still today a strong cultural memory of Catholics being forbidden to read the scriptures. It is hard to trace whether this was ever officially sanctioned or not. Nevertheless, the use of the Bible was hardly encouraged, even though the Douay Bible (1582–1610) was published just before its more famous contemporary, the King James Bible (1611). As a matter of course in those days, the reading of Protestant versions was forbidden. So, whether formal or not, the direct use of the Word of God unfortunately was not a mark of Catholic spirituality for some centuries. The major turn around (illustrated in the vignette of Pope Francis) is the fruit of several movements in the twentieth century, the Second Vatican Council and the teachings of all the popes since that Council. The most visible evidence for the ordinary believer has been the post-conciliar lectionary, with its greatly increased selection of biblical readings.

The Sunday Lectionary[1]

In the early twentieth century, three movements had a particular impact: ecumenism, the liturgical movement and the biblical theology movement. All three found their place at Vatican II and influenced the understanding of scripture and its place in the worshipping community. The evidence of the change

1. I am grateful to my friend and colleague Dr Tom Whelan (Milltown Institute, Dublin) for drawing my attention to Normand Bonneau's work: *The Sunday Lectionary: Ritual Word, Paschal Shape* (Collegeville, MN: The Liturgical Press, 1998).

is apparent every Sunday by communities using the Catholic Lectionary or the Revised Common Lectionary.

Until then all the traditions had their own sequence of readings, usually a one-year cycle. Statistics will not express everything, but in this case they are eloquent. In the Tridentine Lectionary, generally, there were two readings from the New Testament – the Epistle and the Gospel. How much of the Bible was used? In fact, surprisingly little.[2] It is instructive to note that there was no 'lectionary' in the form of a book or books. Instead, because the readings were few, they were conveniently incorporated into the Roman Missal of those days.

Counting the readings used on Sundays, vigils and major feasts, the ordinary Catholic (with a missal in English) would have heard this much scripture:

	Total verses	Verses in the Missal	Percentage in the Missal
NT Gospels	3,772	848	22.4%
NT Epistles	4,178	461	11%
Old Testament[3]	25,044	255	1.02%

The breakdown of use of the Gospels is striking:

	Matthew	Mark	Luke	John
Sundays	21	3	18	12
Vigils etc.	5	1	3	8
Total	26	4	21	20

---

2. I have benefited greatly from the compendious website of Felix Just SJ. Here is the source for these statistics: http://catholic-resources.org/Lectionary/Roman_Missal.htm.

3. The Old Testament was aired especially in Lent, Holy Week and the Easter Triduum.

The prominence given to Matthew and the neglect of Mark reflect the patristic and traditional understanding that Mark was a subsequent abbreviation of Matthew. It can still surprise, given the attention accorded to Mark over the last two-and-half centuries of scholarship.

The 1969 lectionary was greatly enriched, as even the following bare statistics indicate.

	Total verses	Lectionary verses	Lectionary percentage
NT Gospels	3,772	2,184	57.8%
NT Epistles	4,178	1,063	25.4%
Old Testament[4]	25,044	932	3.7%

Given that the readings are spread over a three-year cycle, the actual quantity of the New Testament read on any given Sunday is more or less the same. The major difference is that nearly two-thirds of all the Gospels are read over the three-year cycle. This does contrast significantly with the previous one-fifth. If someone were to attend Mass with absolute regularity over three years, then she would be presented with more or less the complete Gospels, when one bears in mind the duplicate passages.

In the case of the Hebrew Bible/Old Testament, the change is even more notable. Every Sunday (with seasonal exceptions), some passage from the Jewish scriptures is read. Nevertheless, this still comes to only 3.7 per cent, again over three years. Thus the quantity of Old Testament read in one year is approximately 1.2 per cent, not too different really from the previous percentage of 1.02 per cent. Of course, it may feel as if we are hearing great quantities of the Hebrew Bible, but this is not so for two reasons. First, the readings are carefully excerpted and mostly quite

---

4. Not taking account of the Psalms.

brief. Second, there is one period in the liturgical year when even the first reading is taken from the New Testament, that is, throughout Eastertide and for the day Mass of Pentecost. Thus for eight Sundays, there is no reading from the Hebrew Bible. The reception of these readings from the Hebrew Bible has varied from catechetical enthusiasm to what we may call closet Marcionism.[5] The feeling that we are somehow getting too much of the Hebrew Bible hardly stands up to critical analysis, but it may well reflect the inability of those present to make much sense of such passages without some assistance. This is true of both lay people and clergy.

Finally, even though in the previous lectionary there was always an 'epistle', nevertheless only 11 per cent of the non-Gospel books of the New Testament was read. This now stands at 25 per cent – a notable increase, even when spread over three years. It means we are hearing much more of this part of the New Testament but in shorter 'doses'.

It must be said that this true enrichment of the lectionary was presented to the ordinary parishioner and priest without much help or explanation. For Catholics, it simply happened. It was noted by the experts preparing the new lectionary that neither the faithful nor the clergy had sufficient preparation or training to make good news of this new situation. How did such a revolution take place?

---

5. Marcion lived from about AD 85 to c. 160. He was the first to delineate a canon or list of the books of the Christian Bible. His Bible consisted of eleven volumes. The first was called the Evangelikon, taken from Luke's Gospel from which Marcion excised passages he did not agree with. The second, the Apostolikon, was made up of ten letters of Paul, likewise excerpted by Marcion. The entire Jewish scriptures were set aside. His motive was theological. First, he believed in absolute discontinuity between Judaism and Christianity. Second, he believed the God of the Old Testament to be utterly incompatible with the God of Jesus. Systematising these thoughts form about AD 144 onwards, he obliged the emerging Catholic Church to develop and affirm its own canon. The feeling that the Old Testament is not really part of God's revelation surfaces regularly. It is a mild paradox that the writings of Luke – from around AD 110 or so – may well have been written to counter an already emerging proto-Marcionism.

Composing the Lectionary

The lectionary of the Roman Missal, promulgated on Pentecost Sunday 1969, was the fruit of previous decades of enquiry and research and, more specifically, of five years of the most intense and varied experiment and review.

The background to the new liturgy and lectionary included several significant 'movements', without which it would be impossible to understand how things changed so swiftly in the sixties. The roots of the Liturgical Movement lay in the nineteenth century. There were several dimensions to this. In part, this was very scholarly: the recovery of plainchant (*Solesmes*) and of patristic texts with the publication of the *Patrologia Graeca* and the *Patrologia Latina* (*Migne*). In part it was very pastoral, with the founding of national institutes of pastoral liturgy and the promotion of pastoral theology as such. A great deal of this work was ecumenically inspired, and the Ecumenical Movement itself was part of the energy and vision. In the preparation period, the lectionaries of all churches of whatever tradition were inspected for inspiration and ideas. Finally, the Biblical Theology Movement was a reaction both to the Great War and to the failure of liberal Protestantism. It may be said to have begun with the publication of the first edition of Karl Barth's *Epistle to the Romans*. In the long term, the Biblical Theology Movement did not prosper, but it did have great influence and left its mark on the new lectionary. For instance, the typological reading of the Hebrew Bible/Old Testament comes in part from this movement. The history of salvation approach felt the Old Testament was always straining forward to its fulfilment in the New. The Church Fathers also read the Old Testament typologically, so this was not really an innovation, but it was new theologically. Thus, the intense work from 1965 to 1969 was not without a much deeper foundation, which helps us to understand how so much was achieved in so short a time.

The Bible itself was fundamental to the Second Vatican Council. When the Council came to consider the liturgy, it famously said:

> The treasures of the Bible are to be opened up more lavishly, so that richer fare may be provided for the faithful at the table of God's word. In this way a more representative portion of the holy scriptures will be read to the people in the course of a prescribed number of years. (*Constitution on the Sacred Liturgy* §51).

Some other less familiar citations capture something of the energy and vision:

> Thus to achieve the restoration, progress, and adaptation of the sacred liturgy, it is essential to promote that warm and living love for scripture to which the venerable tradition of both eastern and western rites gives testimony. (*Constitution on the Sacred Liturgy* §24)

> Easy access to Sacred Scripture should be provided for all the Christian faithful (*Constitution on Divine Revelation* §22).[6] Therefore, all the clergy must hold fast to the Sacred Scriptures through diligent sacred reading and careful study, especially the priests of Christ and others, such as deacons and catechists who are legitimately active in the ministry of the word. This is to be done so that none of them will become 'an empty preacher of the word of God outwardly, who is not a listener to it inwardly' (4) since they must share the abundant wealth of the divine word with the faithful committed to them, especially in the sacred liturgy. The sacred synod also earnestly and especially urges all the Christian faithful, especially Religious, to learn by frequent reading of the divine Scriptures the 'excellent knowledge of Jesus Christ' (Phil 3:8). 'For ignorance of the Scriptures is ignorance of Christ.' (*Constitution on Divine Revelation* §25).

---

6. That fact that this needed to be said is eloquent in itself.

As part of the renewal of worship, experimentation with different lectionaries was permitted. For a synthetic view of what happened, the account given by Annibale Bugnini in *The Reform of the Liturgy 1948–1975* remains fundamental.[7] At the request of national hierarchies, experimental lectionaries were explored. A great deal of consideration went into the principles that should govern the creation of the new lectionary. Should there be only two or three readings? Should there be a two- or three-year cycle? Should the old lectionary be retained as one of those cycles? Should there be continuous reading of all texts, including the Old Testament? Should the selection of readings be thematic or some combination of continuous and thematic readings?

The name of Fr Gaston Fontaine has not made it into the popular memory of Vatican II. He provided a tremendous service by creating a vast comparative analysis of all previous lectionaries, ancient and modern, Western and Eastern, Catholic and Reformed. At the same time, thirty-one biblical scholars were asked to select from all the books of the Bible those passages they regarded as suitable/essential for lectionary use.[8] About one hundred catechetical experts and pastors were also involved. A gargantuan process was set in motion, with the goal of fulfilling the wish of the Council that 'the treasures of the Bible are to be opened up more lavishly'. Finally, the *Ordo Lectionum Pro Dominicis, Feriis et Festis Sanctorum* was published in July 1967. Then, some eight hundred experts on scripture, liturgy, catechesis and pastoral care scrutinised the results. As a result, a radical revision took place immediately and

7. Annibale Bugnini, *The Reform of the Liturgy 1948–1975* (Collegville, MN: The Liturgical Press, 1990). Chapter 26 (pp. 406–425) synthesises briskly – even breathlessly – the intense experimentation, research and review of the short time from 1965 to 1969.

8. The full list of names is given by Bugnini in *The Reform of the Liturgy* in the footnotes on pages 412–3.

was finalised through 1968. Eventually, in May 1969, the proofs were presented to the pope.

In the apostolic constitution, *Missale Romanum*, Paul VI wrote:

> We are fully confident that both priests and faithful will prepare their hearts more devoutly and together at the Lord's Supper, meditating more profoundly on Sacred Scripture, and at the same time they will nourish themselves more day by day with the words of the Lord. It will follow then that according to the wishes of the Second Vatican Council, Sacred Scripture will be at the same time a perpetual source of spiritual life, an instrument of prime value for transmitting Christian doctrine and finally the centre of all theology.

The result of this tremendous labour is the lectionary as we now have it. In the end, a three-year cycle was agreed. The continuous or thematic debate ended in a compromise: the Gospel and Epistle would be continuous, while the Old Testament would be chosen mostly to anticipate the Gospel theme. John's Gospel would be read in the seasons of Lent and Easter, as well as supplementing the year of Mark. For the weekday lectionary (not really under consideration here), the Gospels are the same each year but there is a two-year cycle for the first reading. In this way, a semi-continuous reading of some Old Testament books was achieved. As noted, even that is not without its difficulties.

The Lectionary in Practice[9]

As anticipated by those who prepared it, neither priests nor people were able to take in the new richness of scripture immediately. Great efforts were made – *Scripture in Church*

---

9. Cf. Thomas O'Loughlin's excellent *Making the Most of the New Lectionary* (London: SPCK, 2012).

would be a good example of such resources at the local level in Ireland. But because the previous teaching of scripture seems to have been generally less than adequate, and because Catholics were not really familiar with the Bible as such, the effect of the lectionary was muted, initially at least. This is just beginning to change now, some fifty years later. If I may put it like this, in the immediate aftermath of Vatican II, Catholics (laity and clergy) took up the Bible because they were told to. Today, after all the difficulties of recent decades, Catholics (laity and clergy) now take up the Bible because they need to. The shift is significant. There is greater hunger for the Word of God and for the understanding of the Word of God among both laity and those in ministry.

By choosing a mixed approach of both thematic and continuous reading, the lectionary has privileged (rightly) the Gospel. Because the Gospel stories concern Jesus and his teaching, most people find the Gospel more approachable and nourishing. We are all naturally drawn to narrative and usually in the Gospel we have a complete narrative, with a satisfying beginning, middle and end.

Matching the Gospel with an Old Testament reading linked to it has had a number of effects. It first of all strengthens the idea that the Gospel is the most important reading by anticipating in some way the content and message. The Old Testament reading connects either by explicit theme or by typology to the Gospel scene. With a little training and practice, spotting what is going on is not difficult for most people.

There are disadvantages. First, it means that the Old Testament is never read as such and for itself, but always in view of something else. This 'in view of something else' is in tension with contemporary biblical scholarship, which tries to recover the meaning at the time of writing without neglecting the Christian reception of such books. A typological reading, however, tends to turn our gaze firmly away from the meaning at the time of writing.

When we bear in mind that the Hebrew Bible is never read continuously on Sundays and feasts, it may be said that the lectionary constitutes a certain (unintentional) devaluing of the Hebrew Bible. Continuous reading from the Old Testament is not without its challenges, as we know from the weekday lectionary, and yet the fact that we never get to hear the overarching narratives of the different books means they remain somewhat on the fringes of awareness.[10] Perhaps liturgy is not the place for achieving this and I'm not really suggesting that we review the Sunday lectionary to include a third continuous reading, without thematic link to the other readings. I'm merely hinting at some weakness inherent in this way of reading scripture, specifically the Old Testament. Also, the typological reading of the Old Testament, already begun in the New, is a somewhat dated way of handling the ancient texts, reflecting more the patristic period and the revival of interest in patristic exegesis just before Vatican II. Such didacticism of yesteryear does not always serve us well. Some such 'wider reading' approach is necessary, but not always at the price of subjugating the Hebrew Scriptures to needs of Christian proclamation. After all, we still hear on Sundays and feasts only 1.2 per cent of the Old Testament each year. It really is not a lot.

With the focus firmly on the teaching line running from the Old Testament to the Gospel reading, another effect of the new lectionary has been the practical neglect of Paul in Catholic preaching. This must always seem extraordinary. The centrality of Paul's ideas in Christian thinking, and no less in Vatican II,

---

10. A good attempt is made in the Lent lectionary, where each cycle offers a different overarching Old Testament narrative.

reminds us what a gift it was that someone of his extraordinary faith, spiritual intelligence, physical energy and sheer brilliance was at the service of the Christian movement at its inception. He was not the founder of Christianity, as some have in the past and still today foolishly maintain, but it would have been very, very different without him. Given the importance of 'the apostle' for the Church Fathers, the mediaeval scholastics and the Reformers, his relative neglect today, at least in preaching, is all the more regrettable.

A strength of the new lectionary – despite the neglect of Paul in preaching – is that he is read at least semi-continuously. But it remains a challenge to take meaning from what is only a paragraph or so each Sunday. His arguments are like great mosaics – expansive and engaging. In a mosaic, while it is possible that a tessera or two might be jewel-like and beautiful in its own right, in reality each tessera or even each vignette of a mosaic makes sense only when we see it in the context of the overall design. It will be well known that Paul's grand arguments usually extend over three or four chapters. It is also well known that these grand arguments are organised according to the principles of Hellenistic rhetoric. This is so much the case that any single paragraph – perhaps jewel-like and beautiful in its own right – takes on its true meaning only within the overarching persuasion of the argument. When we bear in mind that Paul is offering discursive thought, rather than storytelling, it is easy to see why both hearers and preachers shy away from him.

The neglect of Paul is regrettable for another reason. One of the challenges of faith today is the demise of the classical western understanding of atonement.[11] One of the consequences

---

11. The classical atone theory of Anselm of Canterbury (and its Reformed reception, Penal Substitution) no longer stands up to critical analysis based on biblical studies, the advance of science, the theology of God and the theology of the Resurrection of Jesus.

is that the contemporary proclamation of salvation is without a core narrative carrying cultural and existential resonance. If the ordinary believer (or preacher for that matter) were asked today what 'happened' for us in Jesus' death and Resurrection, a confused silence would ensue. This is perfectly understandable because of the aforementioned collapse of the classical atonement model, but also because the Synoptic Gospels do not offer a clear teaching on salvation and redemption. Of course they tell the story – and in the telling they promote a view – but they do not offer a theology. Three New Testament writers do give us intellectually challenging and satisfying theologies of salvation: Paul, Hebrews and the Fourth Gospel. Paul has, for example, a culturally viable and theologically resonant account: the compassionate solidarity of Jesus, which discloses the faithfulness of God.[12] Along with Hebrews and the Fourth Gospel, Paul could help us build a new vision of salvation and redemption, giving us alternative ways of presenting the Good News in our time.

The Impacts on People and Preachers

The initial impact on both people and preachers was like serving a starving man a multi-course Christmas dinner. It must have seemed all too sudden and all too much. It has taken a long time for the lectionary to bed down; perhaps it is still happening now. Many people feel the need to take responsibility for their own faith, and the Bible is the first step in that project and the best resource. The growth in Bible study groups and the practice of *lectio divina* are both measures of a new interest in the Word of God. The current insistence of Pope Francis on the place of the Bible in the lives of those in ministry implies the recognition of a lack. We read in his *The Joy of the Gospel*:

12. The best synthesis is perhaps Romans 3:21-26 (in the NET Bible translation).

The first step, after calling upon the Holy Spirit in prayer, is to give our entire attention to the biblical text, which needs to be the basis of our preaching. Whenever we stop and attempt to understand the message of a particular text, we are practising 'reverence for the truth'. This is the humility of heart which recognises that the word is always beyond us, that 'we are neither its masters or owners, but its guardians, heralds and servants'. This attitude of humble and awe-filled veneration of the word is expressed by taking the time to study it with the greatest care and a holy fear lest we distort it. To interpret a biblical text, we need to be patient, to put aside all other concerns, and to give it our time, interest and undivided attention. We must leave aside any other pressing concerns and create an environment of serene concentration. It is useless to attempt to read a biblical text if all we are looking for are quick, easy and immediate results. Preparation for preaching requires love. We only devote periods of quiet time to the things or the people whom we love; and here we are speaking of the God whom we love, a God who wishes to speak to us. Because of this love, we can take as much time as we need, like every true disciple: 'Speak, Lord, for your servant is listening' (1 Sm 3:9). (*The Joy of the Gospel* §146)

The new Catholic lectionary was quickly recognised as a major liturgical, biblical, spiritual and ecumenical achievement. A fruit of that achievement has been the development of the Revised Common Lectionary. Following extensive consultations, this emerged in 1994. While following the ordo of readings created after Vatican II, it does increase the readings from the Old Testament (especially the Wisdom books) and it offers, as an alternative, *lectio continua* from the Hebrew Bible. In this country, the easiest way to appreciate the RCL is to consult the 2004 *Irish Book of Common Prayer*. The Table of Readings may be found on pp. 24–70.[13] By way of illustration, here are the appointed readings for Proper 19 (Sunday 24 in Ordinary Time), in Year B.

Proper 19	Sunday 24
CONTINUOUS	
Proverbs 1:20-33 Psalm 19 or Canticle: *Song of Wisdom*	
PAIRED	
Isaiah 50:4-9a	Isaiah 50:5-9
Psalm 116:1-9	Psalm 114 (= Psalm 116):1-6, 8-9
James 3:1-12	James 2:14-18
Mark 8:27-38	Mark 8:27-35

As is apparent, the overlap is great while certain adjustments have been made. A revision of the Catholic Lectionary was foreseen when it was in preparation but never enacted. The hope had been to let three three-year cycles elapse and then to conduct a thorough review and revision. Perhaps the time has come again for the Catholic Church to learn from the experience and commitment of other Christian traditions?

In the mid-twentieth century, many Churches revised their liturgy as well as their lectionary. Broadly, the Churches of the Reform were reappraising their practice of sacraments, especially the Eucharist. At the same time, the Roman Catholic Church was rediscovering the place and power of the Word, in life and

---

13. The previous 1926 Church of Ireland lectionary for use at Holy Communion (also instructive in relative neglect of the Old Testament) is conveniently given in the same book on pages 71–73.

in worship. Such convergence is a sign of mutual appreciation of the gifts of different traditions. It is a matter of considerable satisfaction and even hope that across the most varied Churches,[14] many Christians worldwide are now nourished by a substantially shared reading of the Word of God when they come together for worship on Sundays. It is a kind of communion, impaired but real.

Conclusion

Where to from here? As people take up the Bible more and more, this is having an effect on the continued reception of the lectionary. Unsatisfactory or puzzling readings now give rise to criticism at a popular level. The bedding down of feminist criticism would be an example. Why should we have to struggle with such material? A greater familiarity with scripture also raises expectations regarding preaching. It can happen that at least some of the listeners are more in tune with the Word than some of the speakers. Finally, while some continue to have difficulties with the Hebrew Bible/Old Testament, a more interesting question is coming to light: why listen to such ancient texts at all? This is a wider question affecting our identity as Christians and our rootedness in the classical texts of our tradition. In the meantime, we can continue to enjoy and explore 'that richer fare ... at the table of God's word'.

---

14. For example, the following incomplete list illustrates just how many Churches have adopted the RCL: Church of Ireland, Anglican (Ireland); Church of England; Church of Scotland; Church in Wales; Methodist Church of Great Britain; Scottish Episcopal Church; United Reformed Church (UK); Anglican Church of Australia; Uniting Church in Australia (Australia); Anglican Church of Canada; Canadian Baptists of Western Canada; United Church of Canada; Evangelical Lutheran Church in Canada; Mennonite Church Canada (Canada); American Baptist Churches, USA; Community of Christ; Disciples of Christ; Episcopal Church in the United States of America; Evangelical Lutheran Church in America; King's Chapel, Boston – an autonomous Unitarian Universalist Church in the Anglican tradition; Moravian Church in America; Lutheran Church – Missouri Synod; Presbyterian Church USA; Reformed Church in America; United Church of Christ; United Methodist Church; Unitarian Universalist Christian Fellowship (USA).

4
A Personal Biblical Culture

The preacher 'ought first of all to develop a great personal familiarity with the word of God. Knowledge of its linguistic or exegetical aspects, though certainly necessary, is not enough. He needs to approach the word with a docile and prayerful heart so that it may deeply penetrate his thoughts and feelings and bring about a new outlook in him'. It is good for us to renew our fervour each day and every Sunday as we prepare the homily, examining ourselves to see if we have grown in love for the word which we preach. Nor should we forget that 'the greater or lesser degree of the holiness of the minister has a real effect on the proclamation of the word'. As St Paul says, 'we speak, not to please men, but to please God who tests our hearts' (1 Th 2:4). If we have a lively desire to be the first to hear the word which we must preach, this will surely be communicated to God's faithful people, for 'out of the abundance of the heart, the mouth speaks' (Mt 12:34). The Sunday readings will resonate in all their brilliance in the hearts of the faithful if they have first done so in the heart of their pastor. (*The Joy of the Gospel*, §149)

Introduction

To state it plainly at the start, this chapter is about developing a personal biblical culture. Admittedly, the phrase is a little pompous but it is meant in very practical terms.

We already develop other 'cultures' in our lives. By culture I mean a sense of wonder, a bank of knowledge, skill in analysing and a capacity to communicate both the wonder and the discoveries. We don't think of things in this way but, put like that, many people have more than one rich personal culture – to give some examples, sports, politics, music, a special interest in some area of history, gardening, wine and so forth. With the right question, a vast interest, combined with real skill, knowledge and wonder will tumble out. Mostly these personal cultures evolve quite naturally and unpretentiously according to inclination; sometimes it involves a more conscious commitment.

People in ministry today and those (still) involved with the faith will have certainly developed their own biblical culture. They might not put it so grandiosely but that is what it is. The plea in this chapter is, in the Pauline phrase, to do so more and more. This does not mean becoming a biblical scholar at publishable level – enough is already published! It does mean developing this culture a bit more consciously and purposefully so as to arrive at a competence that is personally helpful, spiritually enriching and professionally responsible.

Wonder

Like all the personal cultures we evolve, the starting point has to be wonder and delight. The scriptures have continued to fascinate, frustrate, delight and challenge Jews and Christians for more than two and half thousand years. They have been analysed from every conceivable point of view, mostly sympathetic, sometimes overtly unsympathetic. Some of the great minds of each age have pondered and probed: manuscripts, versions, languages, cultures, history, ideologies, theologies. The methods continue to grow: historical-critical, patristic, liberationist, environmental, literary (narrative and rhetorical), post-colonial and so on.[1] And studies continue to pour out. People outside the discipline would be astonished at the flow of studies and the continued liveliness of debates. It would be practically impossible for a single human being to be on top of everything published on just one of the Gospels, for example. Of course, there is repetition and no one needs to read every commentary. But there are also sharp new lenses yielding focused and new insights.

The academic miracle of biblical studies finds an echo in our own personal probing of the scriptures. At our own level, we all stumble into insights and understandings hitherto unsuspected. It might be a word in the Psalm or a parable from the Gospel; it could be a discourse in John or an argument from Paul. Just as easily, it could be a neglected insight from the Wisdom books, or a deep insight in human nature from the book of Genesis. We have all had such moments, and they serve to illustrate the fascination with this set of ancient writings. The key is the energy and the continued capacity to surprise.

A Challenge to the Sense of Wonder

Paradoxically, the sheer quantity of scripture encountered by anyone in ministry today can itself be a challenge. The challenge is of both overload and familiarity.

At a liturgical level, for example, the lectionary offers three readings on Sundays and two on weekdays. Anyone using the breviary – and many, beyond those obliged to, do – will be praying more or less all the psalms every four weeks and will be

---

1. A still useful overview, although now more than twenty years old, is the 1993 publication of the Pontifical Biblical Commission, 'The Interpretation of the Bible in the Church'.

reading short scripture passages for prayer at morning, midday, evening and night, as well as the longer reading in the Office of Readings. Keeping in mind that there are also special liturgical celebrations, as well as parish groups dedicated to *lectio divina* and Bible study, it means that a huge quantity of the scriptures is on display. We could go further if the work included school or special groups. It is a lot.

It must be tempting from time to time to treat the Word as just another formula to get through, and that would be understandable. And yet it is still the Word, still powerful and still able to surprise. At the ordinary level of familiarity, this represents an unequalled opportunity as well. Mindful listening and mindful reading will help in keeping the sense of wonder open and fresh.

A Bank of Knowledge

Extensive experience of the Word will benefit from a gradually accumulated bank of knowledge.

(i) Bibles

The basic resource is the text itself and it is advisable to have a few versions to hand:

- ▸ *HarperCollins Study Bible* (HarperCollins, 2006) The text is the New Revised Standard Version, offering an inclusive language translation with extensive notes on the text.
- ▸ *Catholic Study Bible* (OUP, 2011) uses the revised edition of the New American Bible; prepared by Donald Senior and John J. Collins.

- *New English Translation* (available through https://bible. org) This is always updated and fresh. Printed copies can also be bought. It is particularly successful in some 'neuralgic' passages in Paul.
- *The Jewish Study Bible* (OUP, 2003) A terrific resource for the Hebrew Bible (in English!) based on the Jewish Publication Society Translation. The notes on the text are really good.
- *The Jewish Annotated New Testament.* The text is again the New Revised Standard Version, but the notes are directed at Jewish readers and are by renowned Jewish New Testament scholars. The goal is not at all conversion to the reappropriation of their own heritage.

(ii) Dictionaries of the Bible

- *HarperCollins Bible Dictionary* (Harper Collins, 2011)
- *Eerdmans Dictionary of the Bible* (Eerdmans, 2000)
- *The New Interpreter's Dictionary of the Bible* (Abingdon Press, 2009) A five-volume dictionary covering absolutely everything, written with pastors in mind.

(iii) Commentaries

Of the making of commentaries, there is no end! However, certain series do stand out as especially helpful.

- *Sacra Pagina*, a familiar commentary series on the New Testament – now a little old, but still good on account of the high quality of the writers.
- *Berit Olam* corresponds to *Sacra Pagina* for the Old Testament. Reading the New Testament Series is an absolutely excellent commentary for the pastor. It covers all the books in considerable detail. It can be bought in hardcopy, but it is much more economical to buy the full

set and use it through the software provided by Olive Tree Software (see below).

- *Paideia* is an incomplete series from Olive Tree Software or from Accordance, specialising in the cultural background of the history and writings of the New Testament.
- The *New Interpreter's Bible* is a twelve-volume commentary on the whole of scripture, including the books regarded as canonical by the Orthodox and Catholic Churches. It manages to be both academically reliable and pastorally attuned. This resource is in hard copy and also may be downloaded digitally from Accordance.
- I also warmly recommend a series entitled *Reading the New Testament*. The subtitle of the series is 'A Literary and Theological Commentary'. The volumes bear similar names such as *Reading Romans* (by Luke Timothy Johnson). It may be purchased in individual volumes or else the full series can be downloaded as a digital package (e.g. Olive Tree Software). The series is not new but is written by excellent scholars with an eye to the pastoral use of the scriptures.
- Finally, the *Word Biblical Commentary* is very complete. This series is not new but the authors are, for the most part, top-notch. The complete set is expensive but individual volumes may be bought in hard copy form or downloaded digitally (Olive Tree Software and Accordance).
- The emphasis on digital resources is for two reasons. First, digital books are usually more cost-effective. Second, the biblical references in the books are in hypertext. All the reader has to do is touch or click and the reference appears in an extra window. This makes the checking of references much easier and more attractive for the everyday user of the Bible.

(iv) Introductions

- There are very many introductions to the Bible and to the Old and New Testaments. Speaking personally, two stand out as especially helpful.
- *The People's New Testament Commentary* by Eugene M. Boring and Fred Craddock. This one-volume commentary surveys the entire New Testament in a clear, pastorally sensitive way. The writers are not afraid to take on theological questions raised. It is available also for Kindle.
- Corresponding in some ways to the theological project of *The People's New Testament Commentary*, the great Walter Brueggemann has penned many studies, combining penetrating pastoral insight with contemporary scholarship. Good examples are his *Theology of the Old Testament: Testimony, Dispute, Advocacy* and his *A Theological Introduction to the Old Testament* (written in conjunction with B. C. Birch, T. E. Fretheim and D. L. Petersen). Both are available in hard copy or for Kindle.

(v) Church Documents

Since Vatican II, the Pontifical Biblical Commission has published a number of really excellent 'position papers' on the scriptures. These are very good discussion documents raising significant issues not only for scholars but for all engaged with the scriptures.

- 'The Inspiration and Truth of Sacred Scripture' (2014)
- 'The Bible and Morality: Biblical Roots of Christian Conduct' (2008)
- 'The Jewish People and their Sacred Scriptures in the Christian Bible' (2001)
- 'The Interpretation of the Bible in the Church' (1993)

(vi) Bible Programmes[2]

These are many programmes, of course, and not all equally good. For the ordinary user:

- Olive Tree Software – comprehensive range of free and paid modules; it is cross-platform and so can be used on computers, tablets and smartphones. It contains many resources, such as *The New Interpreter's Dictionary of the Bible*. Some out-of-copyright resources are really very dated, but some very good material is available at a competitive price.

- At a professional level, you have a good choice: Accordance (MACs and PCs), Bible Works (PCs) and Logos Bible Software (MACs and PCs).

Skill in Analysing

At this point, we come back to the third of the four 'marks' of a personal biblical culture. In spite of the resources just outlined, it is not really a good idea to start with a commentary in hand. It would be best to try to write your own after a thoughtful reading of the passage in two or three translations. Beginning personally like this might sound pretentious, but starting with the commentaries usually means you will hear only what the commentators had to say. Give yourself some time to mull over the passage. Note what is evident. Write questions about what is not clear. Tick any customs/titles/words in need of further explanation. What kind of writing is this? Ask yourself how does this fit in with the whole book you are studying. Does anything in the text recall another passage in the same document or elsewhere in scripture? In one or two sentences, write down what is striking you at this moment.

---

2. For a wider evaluation of digital and web resources, see www.tarsus.ie.

Having allowed a decent amount to time for your own analysis and annotations, it is then time to go to the commentaries, footnotes and introductions. It calls for a combination of confidence and humility: confidence that you too can do this; humility that you allow yourself to be corrected, if need be.

Capacity to Communicate

Skilled communication involves a lot of factors. At the heart of it lies something that is available to us all: enthusiasm and the desire to get across your own sense of wonder and discovery. When your heart really is burning within you, you will be able to say what happened on the road and how you recognised him. This small book is really about enhancing the capacity to communicate. As part of that, we now turn to three studies of Luke's Gospel. It is hoped that the next three chapters will help you see the benefit of making the effort and going just that bit deeper. The final word is given to Pope Francis, a man who has clearly developed a great love of and familiarity with the scriptures:

> I love my old Bible which has accompanied me for over half my life. It has seen my triumphs and been wet with my tears. It is my most prized treasure. I live through it and wouldn't give it away for anything. You could me one worth $1,000, but I wouldn't want it.

5
Jesus in Nazareth

Jesus no longer belongs to the past, but lives in the present and is projected towards the future; Jesus is the everlasting 'today' of God. This is how the newness of God appears to the women, the disciples and all of us: as victory over sin, evil and death, over everything that crushes life and makes it seem less human. And this is a message meant for me and for you dear sister, for you dear brother. How often does Love have to tell us: Why do you look for the living among the dead? Our daily problems and worries can wrap us up in ourselves, in sadness and bitterness ... and that is where death is. That is not the place to look for the One who is alive! Let the risen Jesus enter your life, welcome him as a friend, with trust: he is life! If up till now you have kept him at a distance, step forward. He will receive you with open arms. If you have been indifferent, take a risk: you won't be disappointed. If following him seems difficult, don't be afraid, trust him, be confident that he is close to you, he is with you and he will give you the peace you are looking for and the strength to live as he would have you do. (Pope Francis, Easter Vigil Homily, 2013)

A few passages in Luke–Acts have become popular through the practice of *lectio divina*. The obvious one is the Emmaus story involving the encounter with the Risen Lord. We can include as well the scene in Nazareth, as offered by the same evangelist, in chapter four. The whole tableau is, perhaps, not so fully grasped but one phrase really touches people: 'today this scripture has been fulfilled in your hearing.' As we pray and enter into any passage from the Bible, our hope is that this scripture will indeed be fulfilled in our hearing. This great passage from the hand of Luke suggests itself, in any case, in a book on preaching.

In our present context, fewer people manage to hold on to and enjoy faith. However, among those still engaged there is an encouraging desire to know more about faith, to own it personally and to release its potential for living. Often, such awakening of discipleship begins with an increased use of the Bible and a desire to understand the scriptures better. This is good news for people in ministry, albeit somewhat challenging. Something 'more' is both needed and expected, thanks be to God!

Luke, in a way, starts his Gospel twice. There is the formal introduction in Luke 1:1-4, followed by accounts of Jesus' conception, birth and early childhood. A kind of second start is signalled in Luke 3, with the resonant dating of the ministry of John the Baptist:

> In the fifteenth year of the reign of Emperor Tiberius, when Pontius Pilate was governor of Judea, and Herod was ruler of Galilee, and his brother Philip ruler of the region of Ituraea and Trachonitis, and Lysanias ruler of Abilene, during the high priesthood of Annas and Caiaphas, the word of God came to John son of Zechariah in the wilderness. (Lk 3:1-2)

These verses, full of important-sounding people, also serve as a curtain raiser for the ministry of an unknown prophet from the backwater of Nazareth. In Luke's narrative, Jesus' ministry is further introduced with a genealogy going back to Adam in 3:23-38. The actual start of the ministry is found in Luke 4:14-30, after the temptation scene. Luke can be quite independent as a writer, making choices that suit his own purposes. For example, the start of Jesus' ministry in Mark is well known:

> Now after John was arrested, Jesus came to Galilee, proclaiming the good news of God, and saying, 'The time is fulfilled, and the kingdom of God has come near; repent, and believe in the good news.' (Mk 1:14-15)

In considerable contrast, Luke omits this fundamental proclamation. There are echoes of it, later in the Gospel, with the sending out of the seventy(-two) but not at the start of Jesus' ministry.[1] In its place, Luke offers us this scene of the preaching of Jesus in Nazareth.

In order to grasp what Luke is doing here, it is good to notice how Mark and Matthew treat this scene:

> He left that place and came to his hometown, and his disciples followed him. On the Sabbath he began to teach in the synagogue, and many who heard him were astounded. They said, 'Where did this man get all this? What is this wisdom that has been given to him? What deeds of power are being done by his hands! Is not this the carpenter, the son of Mary and brother of James and Joses and Judas and Simon, and are not his sisters here with us?' And they took offence at him. Then Jesus said to them, 'Prophets are not without honour, except in their hometown,

---

1. 'The kingdom of God has come near to you' (Lk 10:9). 'Yet know this: the kingdom of God has come near' (Lk 10:11).

and among their own kin, and in their own house.' And he could do no deed of power there, except that he laid his hands on a few sick people and cured them. And he was amazed at their unbelief. (Mk 6:1-6)

The careful reader notices immediately that the story takes place well into the ministry of Jesus. It is in chapter six of the sixteen chapters of Mark. The story is also, as it stands in Mark, likely to be substantially historical. Any story that shows Jesus being limited in some way or not knowing something is likely to be very early because, as the tradition developed, it tended to underline his power and knowledge. In any case, the family list seems to serve no purpose of Luke's and so he omits it. Finally, the saying about the prophet being without honour is also found in Matthew (13:57) and in John (4:44). It does require a historical setting and none is more suitable than that of Jesus preaching to his own townspeople. So for these reasons, the story is usually regarded as reliable historically. Luke's version is, however, another story.

Luke – always free even as a historian – moves this scene to the very start of Jesus' ministry and expands it. The original six verses of Mark become seventeen in Luke, with expansions unparalleled elsewhere in the Synoptic tradition. In his hands, the story has become a kind of tableau that serves at least two purposes. Luke's primary category for understanding Jesus is that of prophet. This is no doubt accurate historically; nevertheless, Luke raises it to a major category throughout the Gospel. Our scene is the first big presentation of Jesus as prophet. Second, Luke's account anticipates the full story of Jesus' ministry and destiny. Thus Jesus was indeed initially welcomed. His openness to those on the margin did trigger great opposition. Even if the historical Jesus did not see Gentiles as part of his mission, his unconditional acceptance of 'tax collectors and sinners' was sufficient to cause offence. The illustrations Luke chooses – Elijah and Elisha – were 'in the air' the time of Jesus' ministry and they serve to anticipate the mission to the Gentiles developed and illustrated in the Acts of the Apostles.

> They got up, drove him out of the town (lit. city), and led him to the brow of the hill on which their town was built, so that they might hurl him off the cliff.[2] But he passed through the midst of them and went on his way. (Lk 4:29-30)

Continuing in a symbolic vein, Nazareth here anticipates Jesus being taken outside another city, this time Jerusalem, to a hilltop to be executed. The somewhat opaque verse 30 is best accounted for as an allusion to his 'going on his way' through death into Resurrection. The verb 'to go on [his] way' is a special term in Luke, indicating the path of the Messiah towards his fulfilment of salvation precisely in the holy city, Jerusalem.[3]

Such a reading helps to explain some usual features. As it stands, it appears that Jesus turns on the people of Nazareth in verse 23 in an unprovoked manner. There might be an implied hostility in the words 'Is not this Joseph's son?' but nothing more. The fierce examples from Elijah and Elisha of his healing foreigners do not reflect the historical Jesus. He really did go only to the lost sheep of the house of Israel, and his encounters with real Gentiles are surprisingly few in the Gospels.[4] The moving out from his own

---

2. A cliff does not correspond to the geographical reality of Nazareth.

3. 'Go on your way' with Jesus as the subject: 2:41, 4:30, 42; 7:6, 11; 9:51-53 (NB); 9:56-57; 10:38; 13:31-33 (NB); 17:11; 19:28, 36; 22:22, 39; 24:38.

4. Usually people mention the following: the centurion, the Samaritan woman, the Syro-Pheonician woman and Pilate. Of the first three, the centurion is the most historical. John 4 is a symbolic narrative and, in any case, a Samaritan is not a Gentile. The Greek Syrophoenician woman from Mark 7 (she becomes a Canaanite in Matthew 15) is a very odd story. It looks like a retrojected narrative permitting the much later apostolate to the Gentiles. Luke omits the story, in spite of his generally kinder attitude to women and in spite of his particular openness to the Gentiles.

religion is a mark, rather, of the emerging Church in the Acts of the Apostles. The vicious reaction is very sudden and takes us to the end of the ministry. This verse anticipated the death of Jesus, when people will indeed take him out of the city to execute him. It also resembles the death of Stephen in Acts.

> Then they dragged Stephen out of the city and began to stone him; and the witnesses laid their coats at the feet of a young man named Saul. (Acts 7:58)

The detail of the city outskirts reminds the careful reader of the death of Stephen. The inexplicable, sovereign escape alludes most likely to the Resurrection. Further echoes are (i) the story of the elusive Elijah in 1 Kings 18:7-12, who is mysteriously taken up by the Spirit of God and (ii) the stories of the escapes from prison in Acts 12:6-11 (Peter) and Acts 16:25-28 (Paul).

In summary, the opening scene in Nazareth expands the same scene from Mark 6 (see below), turning it into a synthesis of the whole mission of Jesus, including his death and Resurrection. The elements are as follows:

- Jesus fulfilled the scriptures, as the Servant of the Lord.
- Initially, he was well received by God's first chosen people.
- The opening to the excluded, continued in post-Resurrection times to the Gentiles (symbolised by Naaman the Syrian and the widow of Zarephath), did indeed lead to conflict and eventually to the violent rejection of Jesus.
- Eventually Jesus will indeed be taken 'outside their town' and be put to death, in reality in Jerusalem.
- But, in the Resurrection, he would mysteriously pass 'through the midst of them' and go 'on his way'.

Historically, we may say there is a solid, if slender, core of historicity. Most evident, however, in 4:14-30, is Luke's literary and theological skill, arming the attentive reader before the ministry starts with an overview of the whole. The reader can also see why it is vital to read the entire scene in Nazareth: the whole ministry is encapsulated in this symbolic tableau, providing the reader with essential guidance for understanding the Gospel of Luke as a whole. Such a reading also helps 'explain' Jesus' inexplicable turning on the audience in 4:23-27. That Luke is conscious of writing a symbolic tableau may be seen from the correspondences with Luke 7. Chapter seven resumes in reverse order the marks of the Messiah announced in chapter four.

On foot of such analysis, it is possible then to understand Luke 4:14-30.

> Then Jesus, filled with the power of the Spirit, returned to Galilee, and a report about him spread through all the surrounding country. He began to teach in their synagogues and was praised by everyone. (Lk 4:14-15)

The ministry of Jesus is powered by the Spirit, which is very important in Luke and in Acts. Already in Luke 1–4, everything is the initiative of the Spirit Luke 1:15, 17, 35, 41, 47, 67, 80; 2:25–27; 3:16, 22; 4:1. Notice *their* synagogues, indicating a time after the parting of the ways between synagogue and church. Jesus himself would never have spoken like that. This already anticipates the openness to the Gentiles signalled here and brought to reality in Acts.

> When he came to Nazareth, where he had been brought up, he went to the synagogue on the Sabbath day, as was his custom. He stood up to read, and the scroll of the prophet Isaiah was given to him. He unrolled the scroll and found the place where it was written … (Lk 4:16–17)

From Luke 1–2, we learn Jesus was brought up at Nazareth (Luke 1:26; 2:4, 39, 51; 4:16). He is known as Jesus of Nazareth (4:34; 18:37; 24:19). To create suspense, the telling slows down and needless details create a delay to whet the appetite.

> The Spirit of the Lord is upon me, because he has anointed me to bring good news to the poor. He has sent me to proclaim release to the captives and recovery of sight to the blind, to let the oppressed go free, to proclaim the year of the Lord's favour. (Lk 4:18-19)

The Old Testament citations are from two places in Isaiah. It is interesting to note what has been added, changed (underlined) and omitted by Luke (italics).

> The spirit of the Lord God is upon me, because the Lord has anointed me; he has sent me to bring good news to the oppressed, to bind up the brokenhearted, to proclaim liberty to the captives, and release to the prisoners; to proclaim the year of the Lord's favour, and the day of vengeance of our God; to comfort all who mourn. (Is 61:1-2)

> Is not this the fast that I choose: to loose the bonds of injustice, to undo the thongs of the yoke, to let the oppressed go free, and to break every yoke? (Is 58:6)

Thus Luke has edited a composite passage, taken from two distinct chapters, and he has adjusted the wording to reflect his understanding of the proclamation and mission of Jesus.

In Isaiah, it is not the prophet who is speaking but the servant, predicted by the prophet. The citation is abbreviated and a threatening tone eliminated. In this Gospel, Jesus is portrayed as a prophet-martyr, whose death can be understood in the light of persecution of the prophets of old (see, for example, Luke 11:47,

49-50; 13:28, 33-34; 20:6; 24:19, 25, 27, 44). The term anointed in Greek gives us our word Christ (Messiah).

> And he rolled up the scroll, gave it back to the attendant, and sat down. The eyes of all in the synagogue were fixed on him. Then he began to say to them, 'Today this scripture has been fulfilled in your hearing.' All spoke well of him and were amazed at the gracious words that came from his mouth. They said, 'Is not this Joseph's son?' (Lk 4:20-22)

The single sentence is emblematic of Jesus as the fulfilment of the scriptures, an important theme in Luke–Acts (Luke 1:1, 20, 45; 4:21; 21:22, 24; 22:16, 37; 24:44). 'Today', the now of salvation, is also a vital component of the proclamation of Luke: cf. Zacchaeus and the Good Thief. In Luke, nothing is accidental: Jesus' very first word in this tableau is 'today'. This indicates that a new time has started, a new era of salvation, under the banner of the liberating Year of Jubilee.

The reaction is positive, with a possible hesitation expressed in the question, implying a claim to familiarity. There is no real hint of the animosity to come:

> He said to them, 'Doubtless you will quote to me this proverb, "Doctor, cure yourself!" And you will say, "Do here also in your hometown the things that we have heard you did at Capernaum."' And he said, 'Truly I tell you, no prophet is accepted in the prophet's hometown.' (Luke 4:23-24)

Jesus uses a well-known type of proverb, with a special echo, in this Gospel, at the crucifixion: 'And the people stood by, watching; but the leaders scoffed at him, saying, "He saved others; let him save himself if he is the Messiah of God, his chosen one!"' (Luke 23:35) At this point, Jesus has not yet been to Capernaum (a little inconsistency that does not bother Luke). In the very next scene, Jesus does eventually get to Capernaum: *He went down to Capernaum, a city in Galilee, and was teaching them on the Sabbath* (Luke 4:31). The saying about the prophet is, as noted above, well attested (Mark 6:4; Matthew 13:57 and John 4:44):

> But the truth is, there were many widows in Israel in the time of Elijah, when the heaven was shut up three years and six months, and there was a severe famine over all the land; yet Elijah was sent to none of them except to a widow at Zarephath in Sidon. There were also many lepers in Israel in the time of the prophet Elisha, and none of them was cleansed except Naaman the Syrian. (Lk 4:25-27)

The argument is that God's agent of salvation (in this case, Elijah) was not sent especially to Israel. The sentiment is inflammatory and unlikely to be historical. As noted, the historical Jesus encounters remarkably few Gentiles in the course of his ministry. The colourful story of Naaman the Syrian makes exactly the same point. It is not without relevance that in Luke (only) Jesus heals the ten lepers and only one – a Samaritan – comes back to give thanks. From the pejorative Jewish perspective, Samaritans were regarded as foreigners (which they were not, of course).

> When they heard this, all in the synagogue were filled with rage. They got up, drove him out of the town, and led him to the brow of the hill on which their town was built, so that they might hurl him off the cliff. But he passed through the midst of them and went on his way. (Lk 4:28-30)

The dénouement is recounted quickly. The time is not now, of course. But eventually, Jesus, the Messiah, the prophet-martyr, will be taken outside the holy city for execution. Eventually, the religious authorities – not the people, in fact – will move decisively against Jesus. But Jesus will continue on his salvific path into Resurrection and thus will 'pass through the midst of them'.

My desire in making such an analysis of the scene of Nazareth is to open up the riches of the passage for the modern reader and, not least, to free the reader from any unnecessary historicism. From this passage we learn a great deal. We summarise under five headings.

Salvation

In the Hebrew Bible, salvation is proclaimed by the prophets in the language of this world – not that of the next! Typically, four points are made:

> Good news to the poor (Is 52:7)
> Release to captives (Is 42:7)
> Sight to the blind (Is 35:5)
> Freedom to the oppressed (Is 51:14)

Jesus' ministry throughout Luke's narrative is thus summarised as the work of the Spirit-filled prophet who brings about the promised 'salvation'.

Jesus of Nazareth

The New Testament uses 'titles' to express and hold different understandings of the identity of Jesus. Usually these are the following: Son of Man, Son of God, Messiah/Christ, Lord. Luke gives a special place to the category of prophet. Why? In part, because this was no doubt Jesus' own foundational understanding of his identity and role. In part also because

Luke's presentation of the death of Jesus patterned on that of the prophet-martyr. This is a mark of continuity with the mother religion and sign of God's consistent reaching out in faithfulness and love. A comparison between Jesus' death and that of Stephen in Acts makes the point abundantly clear.

The Death of Jesus	The Death of Stephen
When they heard this, all in the synagogue were filled with rage. (Lk 4:28)	When they heard these things, they became enraged and ground their teeth at Stephen. (Acts 7:54)
But from now on the Son of Man will be seated at the right hand of the power of God. (Lk 22:69)	'Look,' he said, 'I see the heavens opened and the Son of Man standing at the right hand of God!' (Acts 7:56)
As they led him away (Lk 23:26)	Then they dragged him out of the city (Acts 7:58)
They got up, drove him out of the town (Lk 4:29)	
'Father, into your hands I commend my spirit.' (Lk 23:46)	'Lord Jesus, receive my spirit.' (Acts 7:59)
Then he withdrew from them about a stone's throw, knelt down, and prayed (Lk 22:41)	Then he knelt down. (Acts 7:60)
[Then Jesus said, 'Father, forgive them; for they do not know what they are doing.'] (Lk 23:34)	'Lord, do not hold this sin against them.' (Acts 7:60)
Having said this, he breathed his last. (Lk 23:46)	When he had said this, he died. (Acts 7:60)

As a prophet, Jesus is driven by the Spirit throughout, an important key to the Acts of the Apostles as well.

The Tableau and the Reader

Because the story presents the whole ministry in a richly compressed format, the attentive reader already knows what is going to happen. In reading the rest of the Gospel, the attention of the reader shifts from what will happen to the really significant questions of how and why.

Reading from Within

Such a reading enables the reader to appreciate the programme of Luke and, more importantly, the whole purpose of Jesus, understood retrospectively and theologically. Of course, it is perfectly possible to read the story in a naïve way and still benefit from it. The 'less' naïve reading takes us more deeply into the Gospel project. It is the hope of Luke that we, the later readers, will also find the scriptures fulfilled in our hearing, and that we will find our hearts burning within us as he (Luke!) explains the scriptures to us. It is the role of the preacher to listen and read deeply, to find first the fulfilment of these words in the preacher's own hearing and heart, and so to be able to offer a true word of life to those gathered around the word today.

Pointers for Prayer

1. On all our faith journeys, there are biblical passages that really spoke to us at a particular moment. Recall these passages and give thanks for them. What was it that gave them a special power at that moment in your life?

2. Our hope is that as we read the scriptures we will be fulfilled in our hearing, in our lives and in our actions. How can you listen even more intently, with a heart more open today, so that the word may come alive in your hearing?

3. Even for people outside the family of the faith, the words, teachings and parables of Jesus are attractive and convincing. If you were to name the teaching of Jesus that speaks to you most deeply, which passages spring to mind?

4. The whole account of Jesus' life, ministry, preaching and deeds leads to his destiny at the end. We believe his death sets us free from death and in his rising all who believe in him are raised with him. When did you first become aware of this 'life in abundance' we have in Jesus?

Prayer

God of salvation,

in your Prophet, Jesus the Christ, you announce freedom and summon us to conversion.

As we marvel at the grace and power of your word, enlighten us to see the beauty of the Gospel and strengthen us to embrace its demands.

Grant this through your Son, Jesus Christ, who lives and reigns with you in the unity of the Holy Spirit, God, for ever and ever.

Amen.

6

The Prodigal Son

In the parables devoted to mercy, Jesus reveals the nature of God as that of a Father who never gives up until he has forgiven the wrong and overcome rejection with compassion and mercy. We know these parables well, three in particular: the lost sheep, the lost coin, and the father with two sons (cf. Lk 15:1-32). In these parables, God is always presented as full of joy, especially when he pardons. In them we find the core of the Gospel and of our faith, because mercy is presented as a force that overcomes everything, filling the heart with love and bringing consolation through pardon. (*The Face of Mercy* §9)

Introduction

The Parable of the Prodigal Son has given rise to multiple readings and a kaleidoscope of perspectives. This is really a compliment to Luke and his gifts as a writer. To give a flavour:

- **Relationships:** father, sons, brothers, foreigners, servants and, in an unsettling way, women.
- **Biblical:** echoes of other pairs of bothers such as Cain and Abel, Jacob and Esau, Ephraim and Manasseh.
- **Feelings:** desire, autonomy, rivalry, dependence, shame, jealousy, resentment.
- **Issues:** inheritance, property, authority, rights.
- **Theology:** Jesus as prophetic actor and speaker; the Father as God; compassion, forgiveness and reconciliation; discipleship and inclusivity, fall, grace, mercy.
- **Church:** mirrored here too: divided into two groups, absence of women, rigorists versus realists.

In other words, it's a big story and one could go on. Somewhere in there we must find space for the collateral damage inflicted upon the wholly innocent fatted calf!

Our risk today is reading the parable well within our comfort zone. It is familiar; it reminds us of what we already believe from multiple readings; it can leave us reassured but relatively undisturbed. To step outside our comfort zone, we need to remember that there are three characters, three climaxes, and three narratives. Let's take a brief look at each one, starting each with a few observations about the language.

Steps in the Argument

1. The younger son

The version used in the Liturgy is the Old Jerusalem Bible, not always regarded nowadays as a good version.

> A few days later the younger son gathered all he had and travelled to a distant country, and there he squandered his property in dissolute living. (Lk 15:13 NRSV)

The Jerusalem version renders it as 'on a life of debauchery'. The Greek says, *zōn asōtōs*. Etymologically, it means to live 'without salvation', having no hope of safety, and then, by a transferred meaning, it comes to mean a spendthrift, a prodigal in the King James Version. After that, the son's descent is rapid: from family, country, religion and from any sense of identity. The turning point is his coming to himself.

> But when he came to himself he said ... (Lk 15:17a NRSV)

The Jerusalem Bible translates it thus: Then he came to his senses. The Greek says, 'he came to himself', a much more powerful expression. As you can imagine, that later prodigal, Augustine of Hippo, makes much of this expression: 'Lord, let me know myself, that I may know you.' It is good also to observe that in the religious and philosophical language of the time, to return to your self was a significant part of the language of the 'spirituality' of the day. It is also found in both Hellenistic Judaism and in early Christianity as a step towards conversion, metanoia.

> 'How many of my father's hired hands have bread enough and to spare, but here I am dying of hunger! (Lk 15:17bc NRSV)

The Jerusalem Bible resembles the NRSV here: 'and here am I dying of hunger!' The Greek, however, says 'lost', the very same word used of the sheep and of the coin and the very same word used by the father not once but twice. A better version would be: 'but on account of this famine, I am lost.'

This last line is the emotional climax of the younger son's story – never again do we get to see him, so to speak, from the inside. His story is complete, apart from the dénouement.

2. The Father

It is well observed that in antiquity, the paterfamilias was chiefly viewed as the sole source of authority in the household. At the time of writing, people would have been shocked by the undignified running of the paterfamilias. The son ought to be running to him!

> So he set off and went to his father. But while he was still far off, his father saw him and was filled with compassion; he ran and put his arms around him and kissed him. (Lk 15:20 NRSV)

The Jerusalem version has: 'his father saw him and was moved with pity.' There is rather more to it than pity. As often observed, the verb used has both a background in the Old Testament and a foreground in the New. The root meaning of the Greek is your innards; this matches well with the Hebrew word for compassion, which is *rachum*, related to *rechem*, meaning the womb. We hear it in key expressions, such as:

> The LORD passed by before him and proclaimed: 'The LORD, the LORD, the compassionate and gracious God, slow to anger, and abounding in loyal love and faithfulness.' (Ex 34:6)

Remember my impoverished and homeless condition, which is a bitter poison. I continually think about this, and I am depressed. But this I call to mind; therefore I have hope: The Lord's loyal kindness never ceases; his compassions never end. They are fresh every morning; your faithfulness is abundant! 'My portion is the Lord,' I have said to myself, so I will put my hope in him. (Lam 3:19-24)

In the Gospels, the verb 'to have compassion' has a restricted and illuminating use. It is used of God or a figure in a parable such as this one representing God. It is used of Jesus, giving his reaction, for example, to the widow of Nain. Finally, it is used to illustrate discipleship, that is, how we are to be as compassionate, as merciful, as God. In Luke, the story of the Good Samaritan captures this.

All of this means that to speak only of pity is rather weak; this is a much, much stronger expression. The father's emotion is well caught in his speedy and detailed restoration of the son: robe, ring and sandals. The emotional climax, however, is the line, '[the father] was filled with compassion'.

The temptation is to remain with the Father – such an appealing image. Even in the lectionary, the reading is sometimes terminated here, leaving us suitably ensconced within our comfort zone. But there are three stories. Remember the rule of three: once is an instance, twice is a pattern and the third is to break the pattern. One lost coin, one lost sheep, but *two* lost sons.

3. The Second Lost Son

It is arresting that the son who stayed at home becomes, or at least feels himself to be, an outsider, although he is always at home. He is literally outside the house; his natural conversation partners are the servants/slaves. Within the narrative, his emotional climax is signified by the words 'he was angry and refused to go in'. It is significant that he refuses to use the language of brother and dismisses his sibling as 'this son of yours'. The parable does not really end ... the father is still speaking and we are left in suspense. The open ending, a powerful technique, takes us to the heart to the parable.

In some manner or other, the old brother, at home, ever faithful, represents Israelites and faithful Jews, who have always kept the Law of Moses. They could say, with some justification, 'all these years I have slaved for you and never once disobeyed your orders'. The compassion, forgiveness and speedy inclusion of the Gentiles was a shock to them, as we read at the start of chapter fifteen, giving us the context in Luke.

> Now all the tax collectors and sinners were coming near to listen to him. And the Pharisees and the scribes were grumbling and saying, 'This fellow welcomes sinners and eats with them.' (Lk 15:1-2)

Two final comments on the parable may be made. In the Genesis stories of sibling rivalry, Israel felt itself to be the younger child, without rights, suddenly elevated. Jacob, a second son after all, is the father of the twelve tribes. In his anguished discussion in Romans 9–11, Paul brings up the very example of Jacob and Esau to help towards some understanding of the divine project: the elder shall serve the younger. Now the tables are reversed, the elder Judaism has to deal with the elevation of the younger, hitherto excluded, Gentiles.

In families, even rival siblings resemble each other. This is very apparent in the parable. Both want something from the father. Both imagine that acting like a slave will be adequate. The son who transgresses believes that he can return as a slave, as one of the hired hands. The stay-at-home son goes one further – he really lives as a slave. In his own words, 'For all these years I have been working like a slave for you'. Relating to God on the basis of abject guilt or servile loyalty is not unknown in our western Christian tradition. It is instructive that the father rejects both projects and projections.

Conclusion

The parable is aimed at the religious authorities of Jesus' day. The stay-at-home son represents in some measure, all faithful, observant believers, settled, safe, confident and rigorous. Our awkward question must be: who is God asking us today to welcome with the father's compassion? Is it the divorced and remarried? Is it former priests? Is it the LGBT community? Is it the prophets whose voices can disturb the institutional Church? Each of us could make a longer list. The best way to discern is to pay attention to my own resentment and my own resistance.

Pointers for Prayer

▸ Where would we be without our family relationships? They are life-giving and, often, at the same time fraught. To enter the story, it may help to reflect on your own relationship with parents and siblings. Did something of the gracious compassion of the father form part of that experience?

▸ Within the story, there is a lively jumble of emotions. As previously noted we may observe desire, autonomy, rivalry, dependence, shame, jealousy, resentment, but also, loyalty, compassion, fatherly care and even a kind of filial piety, to use an old expression. The conflict can be great and often we simply do not get the balance right. Do I find myself now in a situation of greatly conflicting desires and emotions? How will I discern what God is asking of me?

‣ The chief business of the parable is tackling resentment, specifically resentment directed towards the easy inclusion of others who have not borne the heat of the day. Indeed, why should those awful tax collectors and sinners, not to mention the even more awful Gentiles, simply glide into grace? There are at least two mistakes here and one sign of hope. The first mistake is thinking that the Gospel project is ours or the Church's. It is not. It is first and foremost God's project. The second misapprehension is forgetting that we are all 'in' on account of grace. In the Parable of the Lost Sheep, mention is made of the ninety-nine 'who have no need of repentance'. This is surely, even sharply, ironic. Those who 'have no need of repentance' are simply those who have not yet recognised that need. Finally, the Parable of the Prodigal Son is open-ended. The curious might like to know what happened next. But in Luke's mind it is not what happens next in the story that counts but what happens next in the lives of the hearers of the story.

‣ We don't much care for talk about sin these days, probably because it was so over-empasised in the recent history of the Church. But, whatever the metaphor – missing the mark; falling short; fracture – we do sin. The substantial emphasis of the parable is on compassion, forgiveness, restoration, celebrating and even joy. That welcome emphasis ought not to prevent us from looking at base emotion, ego-centricity, fall, sin and guilt. The turning point, noted above, is very Augustinian: he comes to himself. Such unblinkered self-knowledge is the only path to true inner freedom.

Prayer

God of compassion, you await the sinner's return and spread a feast to welcome home the lost. Save us from the temptations that lead us away from you, and draw us back by the constancy of your love, that we may take our place in your household and gladly share our inheritance with others. Grant this through Christ, our liberator from sin, who lives and reigns with you in the unity of the Holy Spirit, holy and mighty God for ever and ever.
Amen.

7
The Road to Emmaus

I invite all Christians, everywhere, at this very moment, to a renewed personal encounter with Jesus Christ, or at least an openness to letting him encounter them; I ask all of you to do this unfailingly each day. No one should think that this invitation is not meant for him or her, since 'no one is excluded from the joy brought by the Lord'. (*The Joy of the Gospel*, §3)

Introduction

In *lectio divina*, it is said we can read Gospel passages in a new way more or less every time because the context and experience of the reader has changed. Because the reader has moved on, the mode of listening is correspondingly refreshed. This is, of course, true. At the same time, it is no harm to acknowledge the challenge of reading again and again passages that are both familiar and loved. Precisely because a particular passage 'spoke' to me significantly in the past, it can be hard not to hear again the previous message. It is not wrong to hear the old message; but now is now and we have to make an effort to see how the Lord wants to speak today through these words.

Proposal

In this reflection, a very familiar passage will be taken up – the story of the disciples on the road to Emmaus – and explored in different ways to allow other dimensions come to light. Four steps will be followed. First, the question of background and sources. Second, the passage will be examined using 'narrative analysis', a relatively new and fruitful approach in biblical studies. Third, time will be spent on the layout of the story, the pattern created by the author, which in this case is illuminating. Finally, there is no one message in such a story and, as a result, Luke 24 will yield a variety of perspectives on the Resurrection of Jesus and on how later generations may come to Easter faith. Not incidental to the concerns of this book, it is also an exceptionally fine example of how to use narrative in preaching and teaching the faith.

Background and Sources

It may help to read the story in another translation. From the lectionary, we are very familiar with the Jerusalem Bible version. Why not try the Revised English Bible or the New English

Translation? A change of translation can help to jolt us out of complacency. For variety's sake, the REB version is offered here:

> That same day two of them were on their way to a village called Emmaus, about seven miles from Jerusalem, talking together about all that had happened. As they talked and argued, Jesus himself came up and walked with them; but something prevented them from recognising him. He asked them, 'What is it you are debating as you walk?' They stood still, their faces full of sadness, and one, called Cleopas, answered, 'Are you the only person staying in Jerusalem not to have heard the news of what has happened there in the last few days?' 'What news?' he said. 'About Jesus of Nazareth,' they replied, 'who, by deeds and words of power, proved himself a prophet in the sight of God and the whole people; and how our chief priests and rulers handed him over to be sentenced to death, and crucified him. But we had been hoping that he was to be the liberator of Israel. What is more, this is the third day since it happened, and now some women of our company have astounded us: they went early to the tomb, but failed to find his body, and returned with a story that they had seen a vision of angels who told them he was alive. Then some of our people went to the tomb and found things just as the women had said; but him they did not see.'

> 'How dull you are!' he answered. 'How slow to believe all that the prophets said! Was not the Messiah bound to suffer in this way before entering upon his glory?' Then, starting from Moses and all the prophets, he explained to them in the whole of scripture the things that referred to himself.

> By this time they had reached the village to which they were going, and he made as if to continue his journey. But they pressed him: 'Stay with us, for evening approaches, and the day is almost over.' So he went in to stay with them. And when he had sat down with them at table, he took

bread and said the blessing; he broke the bread, and offered it to them. Then their eyes were opened, and they recognised him; but he vanished from their sight. They said to one another, 'Were not our hearts on fire as he talked with us on the road and explained the scriptures to us?'

Without a moment's delay they set out and returned to Jerusalem. There they found that the eleven and the rest of the company had assembled, and were saying, 'It is true: the Lord has risen; he has appeared to Simon.' Then they described what had happened on their journey and told how he had made himself known to them in the breaking of the bread. (Lk 24:13-35 REB)

The Emmaus story occurs only in the Gospel according to Luke. There is a reference to something resembling it in one of the proposed endings to Mark. Scholarship does not regard these proposed endings as representing the mind of Mark, and they are usually taken to be later than Luke and even inspired by him. So no Synoptic parallel serves us here.

In terms of a cultural and literary background, the story evokes other accounts in which a heavenly or divine figure is initially unrecognised. The most familiar of these is the story of Abraham's hospitality towards his three guests at the oak of Mamre in Genesis 18. He is unaware at the start that these are angels (literally messengers). Later it emerges that all along it was the Lord himself.

There is also a kind of foreground, so to speak, in the story of Philip and the Ethiopian eunuch in Acts 8:26-40. The stories do resemble each other: a person or persons on a journey from Jerusalem; the struggle to understand; the self-presentation of a mysterious, unrecognised companion; the unfolding of scripture and the sudden, again mysterious, disappearance of the companion. In both stories you have an account (very brief in Acts) of the good news about Jesus; both stories have to do with later sacramental practice, that is, Baptism and Eucharist. Finally, in later Jewish tradition, there are countless stories of Elijah 'the Helper', who, unrecognised, comes to the assistance of Jews in some kind of trouble or need. Only upon his departure is his true identity surmised. At the time of writing, the ordinary Greco-Roman hearers of such accounts would be quite familiar with divine figures who disguise themselves in their dealings with mortals. Such comparisons do help to locate our story in time and place; they also help to distinguish our story, with its unique features.

Occasionally, readers express a regret that the author did not indicate more precisely *which* passages from scripture are intended. In the Acts of the Apostles, Luke made rich use of the historical books, the Prophets and the Psalms. This is especially the case in the many speeches that review the whole story of salvation. In fact, he does indicate which scriptures, but not here. The broad mention of Moses, the prophets and the writings is rendered quite concrete in the complete work of Luke's double volume. For instance, programmatic scene in Nazareth (4:16-30) makes clear reference to Isaiah 61:1-2 and 58:6 as well as to 1 Kings 17:1, 8-16; 18:1 and 2 Kings 5:1-14. Certain texts particularly resonated with early Christians such as Is 53, Psalm 110, Psalm 118 and so forth.

Did Luke himself compose this story? There are arguments for and against. A close examination of the words used in the story tells us that much of the vocabulary used is unique to Luke[1]

---

1. One the same day, Emmaus, talking, discussing, stranger, in these days, before, to redeem, since, morning, vision, foolish, slow, to interpret, to act as it, further, to urge, evening, to be at table, vanished, to return, to be gathered, to tell, the breaking of the bread.

and a great deal of it is 'strongly' Lucan.[2] Are there any erratics,[3] that is, words that occur nowhere else in the Lucan oeuvre? The answer is no, with two possible exceptions: Cleopas and Emmaus. These are potential indicators of a source because they seem to lack any particular significance, symbolic or otherwise, for Luke. Still, in relation to sources, are the ideas in our story typically Lucan or are there emphases that might come from elsewhere? Anticipating a little, we may affirm at this point that the teaching of the Emmaus story is entirely Lucan in content, emphasis and expression. Given the clear similarity with Philip and the Ethiopian eunuch, we may also affirm that as it stands the story is heavily the work of Luke, whatever about traces of previous tradition.

A Narrative Reading

Everyone recognises the storytelling skill evident in Luke 24. This makes the relatively new technique of narrative analysis highly appropriate and, we may hope, fruitful. To start with, I will provide a brief technical note on (a) plot structure and (b) types of plots.

In traditional narratives, folktales, short stories and even parables, a common outline or sequence is the following. The story begins with the exposition, which lays before us the time, place and the protagonists (vv. 13-15). Quite quickly, it moves to the inciting moment, that is, something is recounted that arouses (incites) our special interest (v. 16). The development of the plot – called the complication – is prolonged in our story (vv. 17-30). The turning point of the story – when all becomes clear

---

2. Going, village Jerusalem, with each other, to draw near, to happen, man, leaders, to be condemned, to hope, to find, alive, necessary, to suffer, glory, to begin, to stay, to be nearly over, day, to bless, to be opened, not (ouchi), to burn, to open, to get up, eleven, appeared, Simon.

3. Erratics in the geological sense: a rock or boulder that differs from the surrounding rock and is believed to have been brought from a distance by glacial action.

– is often called the climax (v. 31-32). Usually, the consequences are told quickly – as here – in the dénouement, literally, the unknotting (vv. 33-35). This pattern of plot can be readily identified in the Emmaus story.

According to Aristotle, there were two kinds of plots: plots of action and plots of knowledge. Over time, a third category evolved: plots of character. In a plot of action, some lack is made up and some kind of reversal takes place. In plots of knowledge, the turning point is an insight, a new understanding that makes all the difference. In plots of character, the protagonist matures or undergoes some kind of conversion experience. In really good stories, all three kinds of plots overlap, as is the case here.

In our story, the turning points in the three plots within the one account are, in sequence:

> ‣ **Knowledge:** 'At this point their eyes were opened and they recognised him.' (Lk 24:31)
> ‣ **Character:** 'They said to each other, "Didn't our hearts burn within us while he was speaking with us on the road, while he was explaining the scriptures to us?"' (Lk 24:32)
> ‣ **Action:** 'So they got up that very hour and returned to Jerusalem.' (Lk 24:33)

Some of the great richness in the Emmaus story comes from the overlapping plots, with their different climaxes and emotional points of arrival.

A final observation, the value of which will not become clear until the next section is read, touches on the number of narratives within the one narrative. All stories are made up of more than one story. This is true here also. Schematically and in chronological sequence, we may note some of the implied 'other' narratives as follows:

1. Narrative of Old Testament hopes
2. Narrative of Jesus' ministry
3. Narrative of Jesus' condemnation and death
4. Narrative of the women at the tomb
5. Narrative of 'some of us' at the tomb
6. Narrative of the pilgrims' moment of recognition
7. Narrative of the return to Jerusalem
8. Narrative of the appearance to Peter

However – and this is the point – in the actual telling in Luke 24:13-35, the natural, chronological order is jumbled. The real question is why do we not feel the jolts of the various perspectives?

1. Narrative of Jesus' condemnation and death
2. Narrative of Jesus' ministry
3. Narrative of the women at the tomb
4. Narrative of 'some of us' at the tomb
5. Narrative of Old Testament hopes
6. Narrative of the return to Jerusalem
7. Narrative of the appearance to Peter
8. Narrative of the pilgrims' moment of recognition

Luke is indeed a great writer; he goes to some trouble to smooth the writing so that the reader is not baffled by the sheer quantity of narratives, missing the main narrative and its centrepiece. What is that centrepiece? To identify that, one more step needs to be taken.

Concentric Patterns
All stories fall into a simple pattern of beginning, middle and end.[4] This can be viewed simply as an ABA* sequence. It is plain

---
4. At least before modern storytelling!

in our story: at the start they set out from Jerusalem and at the end they return to Jerusalem. Often in the Bible, this basic pattern is present in more elaborate structures. Sometimes, the structure is chiastic, that is, ABB*A*. Other times, the structure can simply be longer, along these lines: ABCB*A* and so forth, yielding a concentric structure. There is a question of method here: the corresponding parts must be identified on the basis of repeated and related vocabulary. There is also the question of meaning. It is often the case that whatever it is that stands at the centre is also the centre of meaning of the passage. If such procedures are to take us beyond a kind of linguistic game, then the question must be asked: is the physical centre also the meaning centre?

It is recognised widely that the Emmaus story falls naturally into such a pattern.

A 13 (in the same/Jerusalem/going)
  B 14 (they were talking to each other)
    C 15ab (Jesus himself drew near)
      D 16 (something prevented them from recognising him)
        E 17-19a (he makes a request that stops them)
          F 19b-24 (ministry, death and tomb, no sight)
            G 25 (slowness of heart/slow to believe)
          F* 26-27 (ministry, death and tomb, in the light of SS)
        E* 28-30 (they make a request that stops him)
      D* 31a (their eyes were opened, they recognised him)
    C* 31b (he disappears from them)
  B* 32 (they speak to each other)
A* 33a (in the same/Jerusalem/returning) + Coda: 33–35

The reader can easily match up the steps by reading A and A* and so forth. The real question remains: is the physical centre the centre of meaning? The physical centre is G. that is, v. 25, which deals explicitly with slowness of heart, with resistance to faith in the Resurrection. As we shall see, the whole story explores the different dimensions of coming to Easter faith. In a way, it resembles the story of doubting (finally believing) Thomas: are later generations at a disadvantage?

A Commentary

The reader is directed to commentaries on Luke for a full exposé of the Emmaus story. For our purposes, the commentary will serve the interpretation indicated by the three brief analyses above.

> Now on that same day two of them were going to a village called Emmaus, about seven miles from Jerusalem, and talking with each other about all these things that had happened. (Lk 24:13-14)

These opening sentences introduce the main characters, their purpose and their mood. We are not told why they were going to Emmaus. Given the centrality of Jerusalem for the theology of Luke, it seems they are walking away from the locus of salvation.

> While they were talking and discussing, Jesus himself came near and went with them, but their eyes were kept from recognising him. (Lk 24:15-16)

This is a surprise that gets our attention and ignites our interest. We, as hearers and readers, are further intrigued by their non-recognition of Jesus. Such initial non-recognition is a mark of the Resurrection appearance stories; here, however, it is also essential, for without it, there would be no story. As the story evolves we learn something of what prevented them. We, the readers, have an advantage over the two disciples: we know who this mysterious figure is from the very start. Our attention, as a result, is not on who will they discover him to be, but on how or even if they will discover the identity of their mysterious companion on the road.

> And he said to them, 'What are you discussing with each other while you walk along?' They stood still, looking sad. (Lk 24:17)

In almost any other context, the question would be natural. Here, it is fraught with background and potential. For the wider interpretation, it matters that the two are stopped in their tracks. Later, they will stop him.

> Then one of them, whose name was Cleopas, answered him, 'Are you the only stranger in Jerusalem who does not know the things that have taken place there in these days?' He asked them, 'What things?' They replied, 'The things about Jesus of Nazareth, who was a prophet mighty in deed and word before God and all the people, and how our chief priests and leaders handed him over to be condemned to death and crucified him. But we had hoped that he was the one to redeem Israel. Yes, and besides all this, it is now the third day since these things took place. Moreover, some women of our group astounded us. They were at the tomb early this morning, and when they did not find his body there, they came back and told us that they had indeed seen a vision of angels who said that he was alive. Some of those who were with us went to the tomb and found it just as the women had said; but they did not see him.' (Lk 24:18-24)

A wide review of Jesus' ministry is offered ... to Jesus himself. He is the only 'stranger' who knows exactly all the things that have taken place, from the inside out. The irony is almost painful.

The last phrase – but they did not see him – brings us suddenly into the present moment of non-seeing, although he is right there in front of them.

> Then he said to them, 'Oh, how foolish you are, and how slow of heart to believe all that the prophets have declared! Was it not necessary that the Messiah should suffer these things and then enter into his glory?' Then beginning with Moses and all the prophets, he interpreted to them the things about himself in all the scriptures. (Lk 24:25-27)

As noted above, v. 25 is really the physical centre of the story and the centre of meaning. The story is aimed at countering slowness of heart. Readers may wonder what verses of scripture were taken up and may regret the gaps in the telling. There is no need to worry: any careful reading of the Gospel and Acts will know exactly which verses Luke has in mind.

> As they came near the village to which they were going, he walked ahead as if he were going on. But they urged him strongly, saying, 'Stay with us, because it is almost evening and the day is now nearly over.' So he went in to stay with them. (Lk 24:28-29)

Once more, we are not told why Jesus was walking ahead. It does trigger an essential moment in the story: the two disciples recognise their desire to have him in their lives, even without knowing precisely who he is. They put their desire into very poetic words, which have resonated with readers ever since. 'Stay with us, because it is almost evening and the day is now nearly over.'

> When he was at the table with them, he took bread, blessed and broke it, and gave it to them. Then their eyes were opened, and they recognised him; and he vanished from their sight. (Lk 24:30-31)

The writer evokes explicitly the Lord's Supper and the many meals of Luke's Gospel. It leads to the climax of the plot of knowledge: their eyes were opened and, finally, they recognised him. People do wonder why at this point Jesus 'vanishes'. Part of the answer lies in the genre. It belongs to stories of epiphanies that the moment is fleeting, even elusive. Luke is familiar with such accounts, as we saw above in the story of Philip and the Ethiopian eunuch (Acts 8:26-40).

> They said to each other, 'Were not our hearts burning within us while he was talking to us on the road, while he was opening the scriptures to us?' (Luke 24:31–33)

It is noteworthy that they do not say 'are not our hearts burning' but rather 'were not our hearts burning'. The affirmations in the story are all retrospective. This illustrates Luke's spiritual pedagogy of recuperation. By reading again our past in the light of our present, we see dimensions and patterns unnoticed at the time of happening.

> That same hour they got up and returned to Jerusalem; and they found the eleven and their companions gathered together. They were saying, 'The Lord has risen indeed, and he has appeared to Simon!' Then they told what had happened on the road, and how he had been made known to them in the breaking of the bread. (Lk 24:33-35)

Luke brings the story rapidly to resolution. The plot of knowledge becomes a plot of action, which in turn discloses the plot of character. No longer despondent, they bear witness to what happened, a witness in turn confirmed by the Jerusalem community.

Coming to Easter Faith

As can be seen from the narrative and concentric analyses, at the centre of the Emmaus story is slowness of heart. The story offers a variety of perspectives on how to counter or overcome such blindness or hesitation. These perspectives are not a list of ingredients. Rather, Luke names the typical features, many of which we will be able to recognise in ourselves and in our own journey of faith. A brief comment on each may suffice.

Awareness of Longing ('We had Hoped')

Luke invites us to an awareness of the hungers of the heart. What do we or have we hoped for? Our culture tends to shut down such enquiry as futile; thankfully, our spiritual hungers cannot be so easily stilled or dismissed.

Familiarity with the Jesus Story

Easter faith is built on knowing Jesus of Nazareth, first of all. Even people without any faith can be intrigued by his teaching, his way of dealing with people, his approach to God. The Gospel of Luke offers very rich material for such knowledge and reflection.

Jesus' Story Read in Light of Scripture (Continuity/Faithfulness)

Much like ourselves, the early Christians were certainly perplexed, not to say bewildered, by the crucifixion and Resurrection. To make sense of it all, they went back to their scriptures and looked for patterns and motifs in the Old Testament that would help them understand what had happened. Such searching of the scriptures indicated their desire to see the faithfulness of God, present throughout the Bible, but now disclosed in a highly paradoxical manner.

The Witness of the Early Church (The Women, etc.)

We all depend on the witness of the first witnesses, the women in the Gospels. While the Resurrection itself cannot be said to be historical – 'transhistorical' would be more accurate – the fact that the earliest disciples believed Jesus to be risen is itself a fact.

The Sovereign Self-Presentation of the Risen Lord

Jesus comes to the disciples unbidden and unknown. This sovereign self-disclosure of the risen Lord cannot be controlled by us or summoned up in any way. We may long for him and our prayer may take the shape of deep desire, but the risen Jesus comes to each on his initiative. In Luke's mind, this is one of the features of coming to Resurrection faith, which is well beyond our power to control.

The Fleeting Character of Our Elusive 'Epiphanies'

It is in the nature of intense spiritual experiences that they are elusive. Indeed, once we become aware of them, we move from participant to observer and the moment thereby recedes from view. The Emmaus story accurately reflects this dimension of the spiritual journey.

The Key Role of Our Desire ('Stay with Us …')

In our narrative reading, it was noticed that in the earlier part, Jesus stops the disciples in their tracks. This is matched by a more significant later moment. As Jesus seems to be walking out of their lives, they stop him. They desire to have him in their lives. This is a key insight of Luke as spiritual guide. It is not enough to have all the information; it is not enough even to have had an intense spiritual encounter; rather, the desire for Jesus and the conscious assent in choosing him mark a critical moment in coming to faith and especially to Easter faith.

The Celebration of the Risen Lord in the Breaking of the Bread

In the Acts of the Apostles, the breaking of the bread sustains the faith of the community as we see in Acts 2:42; 10:41; 20:7 and 27:35. In yet another review of the ministry, life and destiny of Jesus, Luke goes on to add:

> We are witnesses to all that he did both in Judea and in Jerusalem. They put him to death by hanging him on a tree; but God raised him on the third day and allowed him to appear, not to all the people but to us who were chosen by God as witnesses, and who ate and drank with him after he rose from the dead. (Acts 10:39-41)

Thus, the continued memorial of the Lord's Supper and the recognition of him in the breaking of the bread are together essential for nourishing the faith of all disciples.

The Confirmation of the Faith through the Experience of the Community

No one can be a believer alone. This is literally true in a primitive sense: I do not invent the tradition. Rather, I am part of a great cloud of witnesses. Luke describes the sharing and confirmation of experiences. This is exactly what happens in *lectio divina*. We bring our experience to bear; we entrust it to others; we learn of their experiences. Together, in the Pauline phrase, we are mutually encouraged by each others' faith (Rm 1:12). Thus the body of Christ, the tangible community of believers, is built up.

The Power of Retrospective Reflection

Lastly, Luke invites us to the practice of recuperation of the past. While we are in the midst of something, it can be impossible to be aware of all dimensions or even conscious of what is 'really' happening. It is only later as we look back and we come to recognise the patterns, the impulses and the motifs, that we being to make our own the very things that were happening all unbeknownst in our own lives.

Conclusion

From a critical studies point of view, the Emmaus story as found in Luke 24 functions as a catechetical tool in guiding later generations to Easter faith. The story is very powerful, in part because of all the layers of telling. It speaks to us today and invites us not to be amazed that something wonderful happened in the past, but to be open to the truly wonderful potential of the present moment.

Pointers for Prayer

- The feeling of disappointment and loss of energy and direction is common enough. As I reflect on this Gospel, can I identify with the disciples going in the 'wrong' direction? How did it feel? Who were my companions?

- The gift of the stranger can be true on two levels. There is the grace of new friendship when an acquaintance becomes a true and trusted friend. This also happens on the spiritual level. It can happen that all along 'he' was with me, although I did not recognise him. Gradually, there are moments of insight and ownership, even an acknowledgement that my heart is burning within me.

- New experiences lead us to read scripture in a new, more open way. At the same time, the scriptures can help me recognise what is happening in my life. Both dimensions are true for the disciples in this story and both can also be true for me. Can I name an experience that opened the Bible for me in a new way? Can I name any passage of scripture that helped me discern what was going for me at a particular time in my life?

- There is both comfort and energy in the recognition that we are not alone, even on the faith journey. The disciples on the road find their special experience confirmed by the faith of the community. When have I encountered and known this experience as a source of strength?

Prayer

O God of mystery, out of death you delivered Christ Jesus, and he walked in hidden glory with his disciples. Stir up our faith, that our hearts may burn within us at the sound of his word, and our eyes be opened to recognise him in the breaking of the bread. Grant this through Jesus Christ, the first-born from the dead, who lives and reigns with you in the unity of the Holy Spirit, God for ever and ever.

Amen.

Soli Deo gloria

Afterword

These few pages have been put together in order to enthuse and encourage the users of the Bible, especially those who preach the Word.

Preaching is a calling and a great ministry. My own experience tells me that people are ready these days for something substantial. That does not have to mean technical or impenetrable, just substantial. It does take work and time. It also takes a good while to find your own 'voice' as a preacher. The main thing is to continue to reflect critically, to experiment and to be patient with yourself. Above all, always begin with some kind of *lectio* so that your 'teaching' rises from within yourself and from within the Word itself.

Index of Biblical Citations